Colonial America

A Captivating Guide to the Colonial History of the United States and How Immigrants of Countries Such as England, Spain, France, and the Netherlands Established Colonies

Free Bonus from Captivating History (Available for a Limited time)

Hi History Lovers!

Now you have a chance to join our exclusive history list so you can get your first history ebook for free as well as discounts and a potential to get more history books for free! Simply visit the link below to join.

Captivatinghistory.com/ebook

Also, make sure to follow us on Facebook, Twitter and Youtube by searching for Captivating History.

Contents

Introduction

The colonial period of American history lasted almost three hundred years. It saw discoveries, revolution, and the shaping of a future country. From 1492 to about 1763, several countries made their play for the land. France, Spain, and England all attempted to plant their flag on the North American continent.

Each country staked a claim, but it seems that England was the true victor, at least in regards to the modern United States. But ultimately, the pioneering, inventive, and scrappy colonists earned their freedom and rights to the land. The road to revolution began in 1763. To their credit, the colonists attempted to compromise with Britain before rebelling against it.

However, to fully understand colonial America and the colonists' road to revolution, it's important to cover what happened before even Jamestown was settled in 1607.

Spain first made inroads in North America. Its territories in what would become the United States of America consisted of the southern portion, such as Florida, New Mexico, and California. France was the next to enter the picture, but it never held much compared to Spain and England, which was the next large power to arrive on the scene.

Once the door opened for the English to sail to the New World, religion became a big reason Englishmen risked their lives on the seas. As the Puritan movement gained steam and the Church of England grew in opposition to it, the new land turned into an opportunity for the bravest of souls.

By 1790, the British population in the United States was quite large. It stood at 66.3 percent with just over 2.6 million people. After that, there were the German, Irish, Dutch, and French, who were all in the single digits percentage-wise. In terms of religion, the makeup depended on the location. By 1775, 575,000 individuals identified as Congregationalists in New England. The Quaker population stood at forty thousand, and the vast majority of them lived in Pennsylvania, New Jersey, and Delaware.

In time, the Kingdom of Great Britain (which was established in 1707, replacing the Kingdom of England) realized that settling the colonies and protecting the colonists was an expensive task. To raise funds to cover its debts, Britain raised taxes on the colonists. Britain had the right to do this; after all, it had protected its interests and the colonists against the French, Spanish, other mercenaries, and Native Americans. However, the colonists had tasted freedom, and they enjoyed it. They had become accustomed to their new way of life, and they had put in the effort to build their infrastructure. To them, they were as independent and free as the Englishmen who still roamed England.

When Christopher Columbus sailed the ocean blue, it's doubtful that even he knew what would come after him. He was going to unleash a flurry of explorations, battles, and a republic that still stands as the world's beacon of freedom today.

Explore American history with us. Dive into the colonial period one more time, and remember where the United States got its start.

Chapter 1 – The Beginning

Before the land became the United States, it was known as the Thirteen Colonies. Those colonies first took shape in the early 1600s with the settlement of Jamestown in 1607, which was a part of the Colony of Virginia. The Thirteen Colonies would continue to take shape throughout the 17th and 18th centuries, with Georgia being the last colony to be founded in 1732.

However, before the Thirteen Colonies were even established, the land was up for grabs. Several powers attempted to claim it, including even the Netherlands and Sweden, although their power did not last as long as the heavy-hitters, such as England and France.

It's fair to extend American colonial history to 1492, as this will help the reader understand why the establishment of Jamestown didn't solidify England as the world's superpower. In 1607, when Jamestown was founded, France, Spain, and England were still competing for that title.

In addition, although Britain dominated the settling of the land that would one day become the United States, the battles within Britain and against France and Spain never stopped. Britain stood as the world's top dog, but the other powers never stopped attempting to topple it. France likely knew that the most impactful thing it could do was take its rival deeper into debt, which it did. France never missed an opportunity to poke at Britain financially and defense-wise. After all, it was France that funded the Thirteen Colonies during the Revolutionary War.

A lot of exploring took place between the late 1400s and the early 1600s that is relevant to colonial America. France, England, and Spain, among other countries, had economic reasons for attempting to expand their empires. For example, Spain sought to amplify its trade capacity and spread the Catholic religion. What follows is a brief snapshot of what took place during the Age of Discovery.

The Early Days of the Age of Discovery

Trade between Europe and the East, which included countries like China and India, had been on the rise since the mid-13th century. Individuals started to see new textiles, goods (namely spices), and cultures, and they wanted more. To improve trade, one Italian explorer named Christopher Columbus aimed to find a better trade route to the Far East by sailing west.

Christopher Columbus set sail on August 3rd, 1492, with financial help from the Spanish Crown. That October, he stepped foot in the Bahamas—he had found the Americas. However, he did not know this; he believed he had found East Asia. On his third voyage to the New World, he would take his first steps on the North American mainland, namely Venezuela in South America. (It should be noted that Columbus did not discover mainland North America in the literal sense. The Viking Leif Eriksson had landed on the continent five hundred years earlier.)

When Columbus made it back to Spain, others saw that it could be done. Discovering new lands was possible. This set off the rivalry between Spain, England, and France.

Italian John Cabot attempted his first trip in 1497 under the sponsorship of King Henry II of England, landing on the coast of what is believed to be Newfoundland. He claimed the land for

England, although, at the time, both Cabot and Columbus thought they were looking at the land of Asia. Cabot returned to North America again in 1498, but his fate after this remains unknown.

Amerigo Vespucci gets the credit for realizing that the land these explorers were looking at was not Asia. It is believed that he realized this in 1501 when he landed in Brazil. A cartographer in 1507 called these new lands South and North America, giving Amerigo the credit for making this discovery.

Vasco Núñez de Balboa was inspired by Christopher Columbus, and he first explored the New World in 1500. However, his best-known achievement happened in 1513. Balboa, a Spanish conquistador, was the first European to see the Pacific Ocean from this new land. Although his trip did not receive royal sponsorship, he claimed the ocean (then called the South Sea) for Spain. Like other Spanish explorers, Balboa was interested in finding gold.

Juan Ponce de León also searched for gold, as well as the Fountain of Youth, at least according to stories told about him. He was an avid explorer of North America, and he even traveled with Columbus on one of his expeditions. In 1513, Ponce de León led an official exploration of what is now Florida. In fact, he gave the state its name, as he called it La Florida. He also became the first governor of Puerto Rico. Ponce de León shows a common theme among the explorers of this era. The expeditions were often funded to find gold and other riches; however, the explorers tended to run into new lands and natives.

The exchanges between natives oftentimes turned hostile during this period of time, but there were occasions when peaceful communication took place. For instance, Juan Ponce de León used the natives as a source of slave labor, which was something explorers often did back then. This likely stemmed from the fact that the natives did not practice the same religion as the explorers and that their ways seemed "backward." The French, on the other hand, tended to befriend the Native Americans while exploiting their rivalries with other tribes to their advantage. It is also important to note that disease devastated the Native American population since they did not have immunities to European diseases. It is thought that beginning with Columbus's arrival in the New World, around 90 percent of Native Americans died, with most of that being due to epidemics of smallpox, cholera, and other diseases, although violence certainly played a role as well.

One of the greatest voyages that took place during the Age of Discovery was when Portuguese Ferdinand Magellan sought to circumnavigate the globe. He was tasked by the Spanish Crown to find a new route to the East Indies, and he set sail in 1519. It's no secret that Magellan embarked on this voyage to gain fame and notoriety for his accomplishments; however, he died in 1521 before he could make it back to Spain to be lauded for his achievement.

In 1524, Italian Giovanni da Verrazzano set sail on behalf of King Francis I of France. He ended up exploring the eastern coastline of the United States. He started in what is today North Carolina and made his way up the coast as far north as Newfoundland.

King Francis I was in a heated rivalry with Charles V of the Holy Roman Empire (he also ruled as the king of Spain and Germany, the archduke of Austria, and the lord of the Netherlands). Charles V wanted a universal monarchy, which means he wanted to be the supreme ruler over all the major states of Europe. As you can see, he was well on his way to doing so. Francis I was not willing to let his territories go without a fight, and the two powerful kings duked it out on the battlefield. But this rivalry spread into other spheres, such as exploration.

Jacques Cartier helped the French Crown gain footing in the North American continent. He set sail in 1534 to discover the alleged Northwest Passage to Asia. The French mariner explored the Gulf of St. Lawrence and parts of Canada, namely Newfoundland, parts of the Labrador Peninsula, and some of Canada's islands. On future journeys, he would sail the St. Lawrence River. He receives credit for naming Canada, which comes from the Huron-Iroquois word *kanata*.

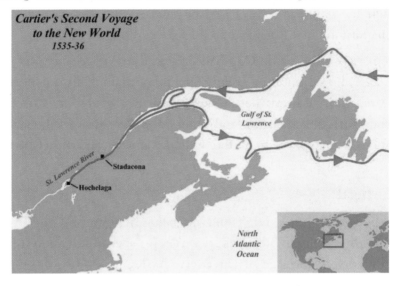

Jacques Cartier's second voyage, which took place from 1535 to 1536.

Jon Platek, CC BY-SA 3.0 <https://creativecommons.org/licenses/by-sa/3.0>, via Wikimedia Commons https://commons.wikimedia.org/wiki/File:Cartier_Second_Voyage_Map_1.png

King Charles I of Spain (the same Emperor Charles V of the Holy Roman Empire) funded the infamous explorer Hernán Cortés, who would go on to conquer the Aztec Empire in 1521. He also funded Francisco Pizarro, who, in turn, conquered another existing civilization. Pizarro made his way to Peru and successfully defeated the Inca. His success helped him claim Peru on behalf of Spain in 1532. As mentioned above, some of the Europeans' success in conquering the native people had to do with the spread of diseases, to which the natives had no immunity. It absolutely devastated their populations, although the enslavement of the people and the sheer brutality in which the wars were fought did not help. Many historians also believe that the Europeans had better weapons than the natives, which is likely true, although some contend that the natives had just as strong weapons as the Europeans.

Conquistador Hernando de Soto participated in conquering Peru on behalf of Spain. In 1539, he made his way to Florida and traveled through the Southeast. In 1541, he crossed the Mississippi River, making him the first European to do so.

Francisco Vázquez de Coronado traveled to Mexico in 1535. Five years later, he set out on a grand expedition, making his way north to the American Midwest; he also explored the Southwest. Coronado searched for gold, treasure, and other valuables. Instead, he spotted natural landmarks, such as the Grand Canyon and the Colorado River.

Portugal

Although Portugal didn't end up being a power in what would become the United States, it deserves a special mention for its contributions to the Age of Discovery. As France and Spain tried to outdo each other, Portugal remained a player in the game too. Before the Portuguese made inroads in the New World, word of Columbus's travels and discoveries reached them. On June 7th, 1494, the Treaty of Tordesillas was signed between Spain and Portugal. Portugal planned to make major inroads in the New World, and Spain agreed to the treaty, knowing its fleet could not match Portugal's. The Treaty of Tordesillas divided the world, with Portugal taking control of undiscovered lands east of the line, while Spain would take the lands that were west of it. Lands that had already been claimed by either country would remain theirs because they believed that they could profit by establishing trading posts in coastal Africa. This agreement was, for the most part, respected by Spain and Portugal, but the other countries did not recognize it.

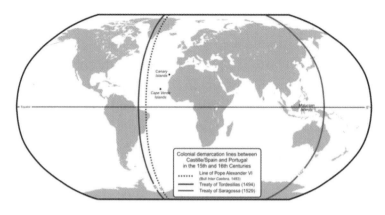

The western line is from the Treaty of Tordesillas, while the eastern line is from the Treaty of Zaragoza (Saragossa), which was the median that split the Far East between the two countries.

Lencer, CC BY-SA 3.0 <http://creativecommons.org/licenses/by-sa/3.0/>, via Wikimedia Commons https://commons.wikimedia.org/wiki/File:Spain_and_Portugal.png

Nevertheless, Portugal saw its own heyday. For instance, the Portuguese captured Ceuta in North Africa in 1415. They soon realized that improved ships would improve their ability to travel. The Portuguese made several contributions to maritime technology, including advanced ships, navigation techniques, and collecting oceanography data. It should also be noted that Columbus spent around a decade training in Portugal before he received financing for his voyage from Spain. In fact, he first sought funding from the Portuguese Crown before turning to Spain.

In 1488, before Columbus set sail, Portuguese explorer Bartolomeu Dias became the first European to travel around the southern tip of Africa, which was no doubt an inspiration to many explorers. The Portuguese also sailed to Africa, India, China, and other areas of Asia, with their travels beginning in the early 1400s. During the 15th century, trade increased, becoming global. Moreover, Portugal faced no competition until the Spanish Crown funded Columbus, allowing it to become a wealthy power.

In 1517, when Martin Luther started the Protestant Reformation, things began to change. During the European Age of Discovery, religion remained a present factor in why people moved to the Americas. But all good things come to an end, and they did for Portugal as well. The world power suffered significant military defeats in Africa under King Sebastian. In 1580, King Henry of Portugal, Sebastian's great uncle, passed away. This meant that the throne had a vacancy. Philip II of Spain claimed it for himself, stating he had a right to it because he had Portuguese blood.

Portugal attempted to regain its independence and began to break away in 1640. England, Holland, and France used the idea of the Black Legend to strip Spain and Portugal of lands left in their control. The Black Legend was anti-Spanish propaganda that the other major countries disseminated. The propaganda claimed that the Spanish were cruel and intolerant. It is interesting to note that the other major European powers pointed out how cruel the Spanish were to the Native Americans when all of them were guilty of doing so. As far as we know, Spain was the first country to pass laws that protected the natives, something that was, of course, not mentioned in this propaganda. In addition, the Spanish Black Legend made the Spanish discoveries seem minor, even though they were ground-breaking, and it diminished the Catholic Church.

The Competitors for North America: England and Spain

When you study history, it's easy to see how power shifted from one empire to another. While you're living history, though, it's tough to see the forest for the trees.

Then there was the relationship between England and Spain.

England and Spain remained allies for several years. However, the low-key rivalry heated up after Queen Elizabeth I took the throne in 1558. As a Protestant, she differed from Catholic Spain, and as a result, the relationship between England and Spain was strained. However, Protestantism unified England. The arts flourished during Elizabeth's rule, and moreover, England found a way to defeat the Spanish Armada in 1588.

History shows that the Spanish overplayed their hand. Up to this point, England remained the underdog. Thanks to the queen's financing choices, the Royal Navy remained healthy. In fact, in the process, they established the greatest navy the world had seen at that time. The fleet saw new life as shipbuilders placed large guns on them. Queen Elizabeth's investment in the navy allowed the country to build up its defense. Without pushing back against Spain, the English travels to the New World would have seen further delays and opposition.

Francis Drake marked the beginning of England's efforts to push back against the Spanish Empire. He circumnavigated the globe, with his expedition lasting around three years (1577–1580). His travels took him to the West Indies. When he neared Mexico, he attacked Spanish settlements and ships, taking the plunder back to England. Although the Spanish arrived at the Pacific Ocean first, Drake became the first Englishman to see it.

Queen Elizabeth greatly favored Drake for his work on the high seas, granting him a knighthood in 1581. Mayorships and governorships were also common rewards conquistadors and explorers received for their successful trips, and in that same year, Drake became the mayor of Plymouth, England. Although there were plenty of lands to still explore, the conquistadors and explorers wanted to get there first.

Thus, the rivalry between England and Spain intensified. When the English arrived in parts of the New World where the Spanish were already exploring, skirmishes broke out. In 1586, Elizabeth I prepared to push back against Spanish retaliation. With an estimated thirty ships, Drake took care of the Spanish at Cádiz for over thirty-six hours. Researchers believe that Britain felt that a war with Spain could not be avoided. Thus, they struck first. Drake entered Cádiz and surprised the Spanish who stood guard. By raiding Spanish resources, the English successfully weakened the Spanish position. When the

Spanish Armada reached the English Channel in 1588, it was considerably weaker.

Defeating the Spanish Armada marked the turning point for England. The English could journey to the New World without the Spanish acting as a barrier. Plus, the English landed in the north, whereas the Spanish explored the southern areas of the Americas.

Sir Humphrey Gilbert receives credit for his ability to develop tactful plans of colonization. He served under Queen Elizabeth I as early as 1566. A year later, Gilbert began developing plans to colonize Ireland. Then he was tasked with attempting to colonize America. However, he was unable to make any permanent settlements in the Americas, although he did claim Newfoundland for England.

Sir Walter Raleigh, who was related to Gilbert, also served under Queen Elizabeth I. He accomplished several feats, including becoming the governor of Jersey, a small island off the coast of Normandy. In many ways, Raleigh set up the first English settlement in the New World: Roanoke. He entrusted the settlement to an explorer and cartographer named John White, but unfortunately for England, the settlement did not work out (this settlement will be explored in more depth in the next chapter).

These explorations paint the broad strokes of what would become the future Thirteen Colonies. To understand colonial America, it's important to understand the rivalries that took place between England, France, and Spain. Had the English not pushed back against Spain, North America might look very different today.

Part of the desire to expand to the New World came from the growing populations in Europe. For instance, by 1600, England had a population of over four million. The growing population led to unemployment, lack of sufficient food supplies, and crowded lands. This led to tensions between the people, which was only exacerbated by religion.

London saw their countrymen turn into beggars on the streets. Plus, the cards were stacked against families that had more than one son. By law, only the eldest son inherited the family's land and estate. Therefore, the younger males had to fend for themselves in other ways.

Exploring the New World provided a viable solution. It also meant that they could compete on the world stage.

However, the English could not have imagined what awaited them. They also could not have imagined what their explorations would unleash.

Chapter 2 – The Thirteen Colonies: A Brief Overview

The Spanish conquistadors conquered their way through the land that became Mexico and other parts of Central America. They also made their way through the modern United States of America's southern regions, which included California, Texas, and Florida, to name a few.

While England watched Spain spread out and take control of these new lands, it is likely its people felt envious. Some believe that it pressured the English to stake out some fresh soil too. It didn't help that England made several attempts to settle in the new land and failed.

Sir Walter Raleigh finally gave England something to celebrate, albeit only for a time. Although the English had attempted to settle the island of Roanoke in 1585, the settlement failed. In 1587, the English gave it another shot. John White and his crew landed on the island, which is located off modern-day North Carolina. The expedition was backed by Raleigh. The settlement soon ran into trouble, and White returned to England in 1588 to bring back more supplies. However, he was forced to stay in the country due to the breakout of the Anglo-Spanish War. When he arrived back at the island, everyone was gone. Nothing was left behind but the word "CROATOAN" on a fence. It is likely the settlers moved to Croatoan Island, where they mixed with the natives, but this cannot be confirmed for certain.

As mentioned in the prior chapter, the tide changed in England's favor in 1588 when it defeated the Spanish Armada. The win gave the English newfound hope and confidence. England had at last gained leverage over Spain. The Spanish Empire had finally met its match, and the defeat forced the county to pull back. It opened the road for England to establish the Thirteen Colonies, as the Atlantic Ocean posed less of a threat, at least in terms of Spanish ships looking to bring down the British.

The Treaty of London was signed in 1604 between Britain and Spain, ending the nearly twenty-year Anglo-Spanish War. The treaty didn't change anything in regards to land. However, both countries made pledges to stop capturing ships on the Atlantic. Spain also stated that it would stop seeking to install Catholicism in England. The English hated the treaty, while the Spanish celebrated it. Regardless of their feelings, peace between the two countries lasted until 1625.

King James I of England had started his rule over a year before the signing of the treaty in 1603 after Queen Elizabeth passed away. Even though the country had new leadership, England's need to continue its explorations did not fade. To finance the voyages to the land across the Atlantic, King James I authorized charters for new settlements. Once a company's trip received approval, the members had leverage to raise money to finance it.

List of Kings and Queens of the Kingdom of England (1558-1707)

The various civil wars and throne changes can be confusing to follow. We have provided a handy list here of who was in charge at what time. This chapter is divided into sections, and there is some jumping around in the timeline to properly cover the history of the colonies. It should be noted that colonial history extends past this list, but the colonies, except for Georgia, were established during the

Kingdom of England, which means the names of later kings and queens are not mentioned as often in this chapter.

- Elizabeth I (1558-1603)
- James I (1603-1625)
- Charles I (1625-1649)
- The Royal Interregnum (1649-1653; when England was ruled directly by the Parliament)
- Oliver Cromwell as Lord Protector (1653-1658)
- Richard Cromwell as Lord Protector (1658-1659)
- Charles II (1660-1685)
- James II (1685-1688)
- Mary II (1689-1694)
- William III or William of Orange (1689-1702; ruled alongside his wife, Mary)
- Anne (1702-1707)
- The Kingdom of England becomes the Kingdom of Great Britain in 1707.

The Colony of Virginia

In 1606, the Virginia Company of London received its charter to establish a colony in the New World. Around 104 men and boys headed to found England's first permanent colony. The colony was officially founded in 1607 at Jamestown, Virginia. It received additional charters in 1609 and 1612. In 1624, Virginia was made a royal colony, and by 1775, the colony still had its royal status.

A colony could have different statuses. It could be under royal, proprietary, or charter rule. A royal colony was under Crown rule. Representation came from an appointed governor and council. Those that were under Crown rule received official acknowledgment, and they oftentimes had more of a military presence. A proprietary colony was one that had charters granted by England; the land belonged to the Crown, but the proprietors could choose who would lead. A charter colony was one that had a royal charter but did not experience direct interference from the English government.

The Virginia Company of London named Jamestown after England's king. The ships landed at this site on purpose. Those funding the voyage knew that the land had a few special characteristics that would make a settlement prosper. The settlement was located on a peninsula, which would allow the English to defend it against the Spanish if necessary. In addition, the area was free of natives—they didn't inhabit this part of Virginia because the land was unfavorable for producing crops. It turns out the natives knew best; the land was isolated, and there was no good source of fresh water nearby.

However, it was in England's interest to settle in the New World, and Jamestown would end up persevering, despite the severe drought the English suffered that first year. On top of that, the men had arrived too late in the year to plant crops. Two-thirds of the colonists died before ships came back with supplies the following year. Nevertheless, the men got to work and built a fort to protect themselves against potential threats. Soon after the fort was completed, Captain Christopher Newport went back to England to pick up additional supplies.

Life in the colonies before solid infrastructure was built was rough. The colonists consumed water that was filled with bacteria, which led to diseases and infections that caused many deaths. And if the first settlers didn't die from diseases, they likely passed away from a lack of food.

The relationship between the settlers and the local natives, in this case, the Powhatans, remained strained. The year 1609 through 1610 (known as the Starving Time) proved difficult for the settlers. Due to the lack of food and water and their inability to depend on the Powhatans for such things, the winter became challenging. Estimates show that only around 10 percent of the original settlers lived. In their desperation, the people turned to cannibalism to stay alive.

In May of 1610, ships arrived from Bermuda. Sir Thomas Gates, who had made his way to Jamestown with more supplies from England, got caught in a terrible hurricane that pushed his ships down to Bermuda. When he arrived in Jamestown, he found it in such bad condition that the decision was made to abandon the settlement. The arrival of another ship, led by Thomas West, the baron of De La Warr ("Delaware"), encouraged the colonists to head back to Jamestown and give it another chance. A more in-depth look at the Colony of Virginia, whose story includes such famous figures as John Smith, John Rolfe, and Pocahontas, can be found in Chapter 6.

Mass grave found under a building at Jamestown.

The Colony of Massachusetts

Although the expeditions to the New World became more organized over time, a surefire path to success didn't exist. Some settlers were veered off course, such as the Pilgrims.

By several accounts, the Pilgrims intended to land near the Hudson River in modern-day New York. Weather veered the *Mayflower* to Cape Cod, where they landed on November 11th, 1620. Before the Pilgrims created their colony, the men agreed to sign the Mayflower Compact on November 21st, 1620. Although it took a few months of exploring, they eventually established Plymouth Colony (named after Plymouth, England). The site was cleared, and the nearby hills provided defense. However, this site was cleared because it once belonged to the Wampanoag; the village had suffered a smallpox outbreak, and they abandoned the village.

In the process of finding a place to settle, the Pilgrims came across Native Americans, including Squanto, who had been captured by the English previously but later became an ally of the Pilgrims. Their interactions with the natives were not peaceful, as both sides antagonized the other. The natives had encountered the English before; for instance, Squanto was taken prisoner sometime around 1614.

In Edward Winslow's letter to a friend in England, Winslow details finding food in caves that belonged to nearby natives. The letter also helped establish when the first traditional Thanksgiving took place— November 1621.

Edward Winslow, who played a key role in establishing Plymouth Colony, had made his way to Holland in 1617 as part of the Separatist movement. Separatists played a major role in the development of the United States. They believed that the state had no say in how their churches were run. Unlike the Puritans, they did not want to work with the Church of England; they wanted to completely separate.

Winslow and his wife were among the passengers of the *Mayflower*. However, she passed away shortly after they landed. He remarried in 1621 to Susanna White, who gave birth to Peregrine White in 1620 while on board the *Mayflower*. Peregrine White was the first European baby born in that part of North America (the first European baby to be born in North America was Virginia Dare, who was a part of the failed Roanoke colony). In addition, Winslow's marriage to Susanna was the first on colonial soil.

Since Winslow was not a Founding Father, it is probably why his name gets lost in the shuffle of American history. However, he is a key figure and served as the governor of the colony several times. When he didn't serve as governor, he served as a member of the governor's council. Moreover, he later served as the Massachusetts Bay agent, which allowed him to represent the colony. Like other colonial icons and the Founding Fathers, Winslow left behind several writings. In many ways, American history comes from them.

Like the inhabitants of Jamestown, Winslow detailed that the first winter presented harsh experiences. In March 1621, the settlers made formal contact with the local natives. Although the Native Americans were apprehensive about the newcomers at first, they eventually decided to aid them. Squanto played a key role in this; since he had been captured by the English, he could speak their language. He taught them how to farm the land, which was a good thing for the Pilgrims, as their seeds were not fit for the soil.

The first traditional Thanksgiving was celebrated that same year, and the meal consisted of waterfowl, fish, and deer. It is believed the first Thanksgiving might have taken place earlier in 1619, but this took place on board a ship and was a smaller affair.

Although Plymouth became an English colony, no official charter was issued to it since it wasn't the intended landing spot for the Pilgrims. However, it still operated as a charter colony. In 1691, Massachusetts Bay Colony absorbed it.

Massachusetts was one of the most important colonies. After all, this was where the Boston Massacre and Boston Tea Party took place, two important events that fueled the fire of revolution. The official formation of the Massachusetts Bay Colony began in the late 1620s. In 1628, a land grant was given to a group of investors. The territory was mostly settled by the Puritans, who were seeking religious reform that was not possible in England.

The Puritans played a large role in the formation of the land that now makes up part of the United States of America. They had become disenchanted with the Church of England. The Puritan movement started because they felt the church had adopted too many Catholic practices. Those with economic bones to pick with the English government also latched onto the Puritan movement. In 1691, Massachusetts became a royal colony. A more complete story of the founding of Massachusetts will be told in Chapter 4.

Maine

Maine became a state in 1820, but it was never an official colony. Sir Ferdinando Gorges helped fund Popham Colony in 1607, but it failed. He then received a land grant for territory in Maine in 1622. Gorges attempted to build the land with an aristocratic mindset, but needless to say, his attempt did not succeed. In 1677, Massachusetts purchased the land.

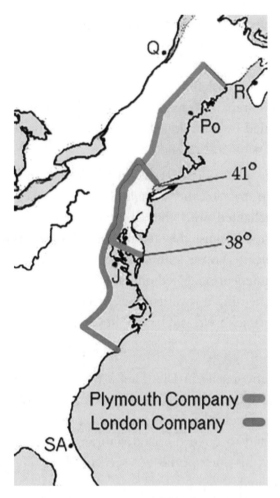

"Po" is where Popham Colony was located; "J" is where Jamestown was located.

The Colony of New Hampshire

New Hampshire was settled by John Mason and Ferdinando Gorges in 1623 and became a royal province in 1679. During these early years, the land boundaries remained fluid. Before receiving its charter and royal status, Massachusetts absorbed jurisdiction of the land from 1641 to 1679.

Keep in mind that border disputes were common while the original Thirteen Colonies took shape. Even today, some citizens of the United States don't realize that borders among the colonies were blurry sometimes. As the colonists worked to establish infrastructure, proprietors, leadership members, and representatives knew that access to water was essential. Access to ports was vital too.

The border dispute between New Hampshire and Massachusetts was bitter, as Mason's heirs sought to claim their inheritance. These disputes eventually led to the colony receiving its own leadership again in 1679. In 1691, New Hampshire became a royal colony.

The people who settled in New Hampshire started an economy based on fishing and trading. They had access to whales, timber, fur, and fish. Even though the colony experienced the typical harsh winters of New England, they were able to set up some agricultural practices. They did not grow enough for trade, but they did grow their own crops that provided sustenance. Common crops included squash, wheat, corn, rye, and beans. The trees found in the colony were used to build ships.

While the Puritans, Catholics, and Quakers sought a place to live in the New World that would provide them the freedom to practice their religion as they saw fit, those who traveled to New Hampshire were often searching for riches. They knew that the fish, fur, and timber trade with England would net them handsome profits.

The colony experienced its fair share of disputes. It seemed to be caught in a tug of war with Massachusetts Bay Colony. Between 1699 and 1741, its governor was often the same as the governor of Massachusetts. In 1741, Benning Wentworth became the governor of New Hampshire, ending the practice of being overseen by Massachusetts. He holds the record for having the single longest tenure as a colonial governor.

Other issues New Hampshire faced were boundary issues with New York. Wentworth began selling land grants, which New York contested, claiming they belonged to New York. Wentworth ignored them, saying that he would only stop if a royal decree was made in New York's favor. In 1764, the British government ruled in favor of New York, upholding the original grant that was given to New York. The Connecticut River became the official boundary. Those who had bought land grants from Wentworth lost their land, although New York representatives were willing to sell them the land again at a much higher price.

The Colony of Maryland

George Calvert, an English politician, sought to establish a space in the New World for Catholics. In 1623, he founded Avalon, which was located in Newfoundland, with the intent to provide a safe haven for Catholics facing persecution in England. Soon after this, though, he resigned from his government posts. He had supported a marriage alliance between England and Spain, and when that fell through, he publicly declared that he was a Catholic. He had been loyal to the king, so Calvert did not lose his favor with him; rather, he was given the title of Baron Baltimore in Ireland.

Lord Baltimore wished for another safe haven for Catholics in the New World after experiencing hostility from the colonists in Jamestown due to his religion in 1629. He received the charter to what is now Maryland in 1632. However, he died the same year, and the charter was inherited by his son, Cecil, also often known as Cecilius Calvert. To help set up the colony, he made his brother Leonard the first governor of Maryland.

Interestingly, Cecilius was very hands-on in regard to the colony's affairs. He gave Leonard instructions for setting up the colony called "Instructions to the Colonists by Lord Baltimore." His main concern was religious freedom for Catholics and Protestants since the Puritans had difficulty accepting those of a different faith.

Many of the early settlers were, oddly enough, Protestants, and they did not run into many issues with the local tribes. In fact, the early colonists of this region owe much of their success to the Native Americans, as they taught them how to plant crops and showed them where to find seafood. To encourage settlement, men willing to eke out a living in the colony were given fifty acres of land for each person they brought, whether that was another family member or a slave.

Cecilius never set foot in Maryland. Since King Charles I (r. 1625–1649) faced so much adversity, the situation in England remained unstable. A change on the throne could easily undo anything that Charles I had set down. Thus, Cecilius remained in England to protect his interests, which were also his family's interests.

It turns out that he had reason to worry, although the problems occurred across the ocean. A privateer named Richard Ingle attacked the capital of the colony and took prisoners in 1644. Leonard fled to Virginia. The brothers managed to retake control of Maryland two years later. Leonard passed away in 1648.

William Stone became Maryland's new governor in 1649. The conflict in Maryland didn't end with him. As a Protestant, he signed the Religious Toleration Act of 1649, which granted religious tolerance to all Christian denominations. The Puritans in the colony thought it was too Catholic in nature. They had to swear allegiance to Calvert, a Catholic, and they believed that, in turn, made them obedient to the pope.

That same year, Charles I was executed; he was accused of treason. He refused to instate a constitutional monarchy, and many viewed him as being too Catholic. He was not actually Catholic, but his wife was. His eldest son, who was also named Charles, took the throne, although he would also face many difficulties as well.

In 1654, the act was repealed. This took place shortly after the end of the Third English Civil War, which saw Scotland absorbed by England. More importantly, at least in regards to Maryland, those fighting for a constitutional monarchy (the Roundheads) won the day, creating the short-lived English Commonwealth. Members of this faction rose up against Stone in 1654 and removed him from power.

Stone attempted to reassert his control at the Battle of the Severn in March of 1655. However, he failed and was taken prisoner in the process.

As you can see, the colonies were an extension of England. What happened in the Motherland impacted them. After Oliver Cromwell, the leader of the Roundheads, passed away in 1658, Charles II was restored to the throne, although he would only do so in 1660. This led to Stone receiving his freedom. The Calvert family rewarded Stone with land granting him Charles County, Maryland. Stone passed away that same year.

In 1729, the city of Baltimore was established, and it was named after Cecil Calvert. Baltimore became an important port that shipped tobacco and grain. Flour milling became an important economic activity in the area.

In regards to Maryland's status as a colony, it was initially a proprietary colony that was overseen by Cecilius Calvert. In 1689, the colony was overseen by the Crown, as the aftereffects of the Glorious Revolution, which was another internal conflict that saw a change on the English throne, saw Cecilius's son removed from power. In 1715, the colony was returned to proprietary rule once George Calvert, 5th Baron Baltimore, stated he was a Protestant.

Map of the Province of Maryland.

Karl Musser, CC BY-SA 3.0 <https://creativecommons.org/licenses/by-sa/3.0>, via Wikimedia Commons https://commons.wikimedia.org/wiki/File:Marycolony.png

The Colony of Connecticut

In 1636, Thomas Hooker, a Puritan minister, and John Haynes, the governor of Massachusetts Bay Colony, founded Connecticut. In the early years, the colony governed itself, but in 1662, it received an official charter.

Hooker is known as the Father of Connecticut. He began his career by preaching in England. Over time, his beliefs began to be more and more suppressed. In the late 1620s, he fled England after being summoned to appear before the Court of High Commission for his Puritan sympathies. From Holland, he emigrated to Massachusetts Bay Colony.

Thomas Hooker was not the only settler who started in Massachusetts and sought refuge somewhere else in the New World for religious reasons. John Cotton, an influential preacher who lived in Massachusetts, was one of the reasons Hooker and his supporters left the colony. Cotton did well at his position in St. Botolph's in England, but when Cotton became the second pastor of the First Church of Boston in 1633, he quickly turned into a controversial figure. For instance, he helped to banish Roger Williams, who would go on to establish Rhode Island.

Several debates involving American history exist, including whether or not the Founding Fathers, colonists, or settlers favored separating church from state. Although Thomas Hooker did not hold the same stern views on religion as the Puritans, he did not advocate for the separation of church from state. Back then, men could only vote if they had been formally admitted to the church. Instead, Hooker extolled the idea that all freemen deserved voting rights. He believed that individuals had the God-given right to determine their leadership. His works helped shape the Fundamental Orders of Connecticut, the first written constitution in what would become the United States.

Another interesting part of Connecticut's colonial history involves the failed New Haven Colony. A Puritan minister named John Davenport led emigrants from Massachusetts in 1638 to New Haven. The aim was to establish a utopia with Christians through economic self-sufficiency. New Haven refused to take in colonists who were not Puritans, which might be nice for the religious side of things. However, running a colony takes more than just faith. They needed people who knew how to farm the soil and how to trade with others.

The colony had other problems as well. For instance, it never received an official charter. Connecticut had one, though, and it was willing to use whatever means it could to incorporate New Haven. The towns of New Haven Colony began to join with Connecticut, and by 1664, all of them had submitted.

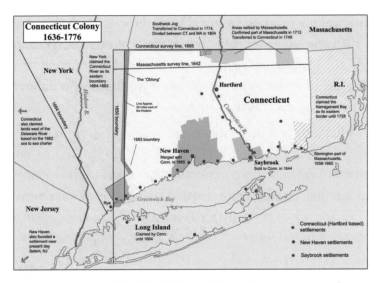

Map of the Colony of Connecticut.

The Colony of Rhode Island

Some colonies, such as Virginia, were founded by investors. Others were founded as a result of disputes among the colonists. Rhode Island is one example of the latter. Roger Williams founded Rhode Island in 1636 after his banishment from Massachusetts.

In order to achieve cohesion among the colonists, they each had to conform to basic principles. To those in charge, Boston succeeded economically as a society because it became a homogenous population. Those who refused to adhere to Anglican Puritan principles received banishment.

The civil authorities took action against Williams and his dangerous views. He believed that land ownership titles meant nothing if they came from England. Instead, the natives needed to grant them to make them official. His vocal opinions on the king and who the land rightfully belonged to, among other things, led to his banishment in 1635. However, he was sick at the time; since winter had arrived, the court agreed that he could stay a while longer if he stopped publicly speaking on these issues. He did not. In early January 1636, the sheriff came to escort him out of the colony, but Williams had already left. That same year, he purchased land directly from the Narragansett. Providence became a place for those who differed from the Puritan ethos, such as the Quakers.

The Quakers got their start in England too. It started as the Religious Society of Friends, and it was founded by George Fox, who believed that faith was more important than rituals. The Quakers kept worship simple. Others made their worship ceremonies ornate and lavish, but the Quakers did not believe that was needed to have a close connection to God.

George Fox left his home in England and traveled, visiting the colonies in the early 1670s to spread his beliefs. He believed that God rested within every individual, while other religions stated that God lived in the church. This mindset got him in trouble. Anyone who questioned the church was subject to imprisonment. Despite this, he managed to form chapters. On the other hand, between 1649 and 1673, Fox was imprisoned eight times.

Over time, laws were enforced that detrimentally impacted the Quakers. For instance, in 1658, Quakers were banished from Massachusetts upon pain of death. Nonetheless, Fox encouraged his followers to continue meeting consistently, and Rhode Island proved to be a safe haven. The Toleration Act of 1689 gave relief to the Quakers in England, as it repealed the laws that had once discriminated against them. Fox passed away in 1691, preaching his views of God until the end.

The Colony of Rhode Island is remembered as being perhaps the most progressive of all the colonies. It even passed the first law against slavery in the 1650s; however, slavery still remained rather popular, so it is likely the law was not enforced. Despite this, the colony is remembered for its peaceful relationships with the Native Americans and its religious tolerance.

The Colony of Delaware

Delaware was initially established by the Swedes in 1638, and it was known as New Sweden. Swedish King Gustavus Adolphus authorized the charter in 1626. He passed away in 1632, but his daughter, Christina, continued the administration of it. Her chancellor finalized the plans, and the company made its move to the New World. The crew landed in Delaware in 1638 at Wilmington. The first settlement was named after Queen Christina. Although the Swedes were not in control of the region for very long, they had enough time to leave their mark. They built the Old Swedes Church, also known as the Holy Trinity Church. It is one of the oldest churches in the United States that still receives worshipers.

In 1655, the colony fell to the Dutch, who annexed it to their colony of New Netherland. Around ten years later, in 1664, the British took control of the region. It was an incorporated county under Maryland between 1669 and 1672. However, the land was attractive to William Penn, among others. In 1682, Penn negotiated a merger between it and Pennsylvania, leasing some of the lands for several years. The merger benefited Pennsylvania because it gave it access to the Atlantic Ocean. In 1701, the leased Delaware lands and Pennsylvania shared the same governor, a situation that lasted for over seventy years.

Even as a colony, Delaware was small. In modern America, it's the second-smallest state but among the most densely populated. It is believed that Thomas Jefferson had an affinity for the tiny colony. Supposedly, Jefferson gave it the nickname of the Diamond State. Jefferson apparently alluded to it as being a jewel. Many believe it has to do with its location next to the Eastern Seaboard. The colonists (and really any explorer to a new land) wanted to establish settlements near water sources. When colonies weren't situated near rivers, lakes, bays, or the ocean, it made setting up their infrastructure a bigger challenge. Luckily for them, there was no shortage of bodies of water in the United States.

The Colony of North Carolina and the Colony of South Carolina

Although the English certainly made South Carolina their home, they were not the first to land in the Carolinas. The Spanish landed there first. In 1526, they established the first European settlement in what is now the United States, but it did not last long. In 1562, French Huguenots arrived in the area. (The Huguenots were a group of French Protestants that had Calvinist leanings. The areas where the Huguenots lived in France were heavily Catholic, so the Huguenots were persecuted.) They spent less than a year on Parris Island before they moved on.

In 1629, King Charles I of England granted a patent to the land, but he placed a restriction on it: land could only be given to members of the Church of England. Since the man who had been granted the patent, Robert Heath, wanted to use the land for French Huguenots, he gave the patent away to William Berkeley, who would play an important role in the founding of other colonies, particularly Virginia. King Charles I would be executed in 1649. Heath's heirs sought the patent for themselves, but Charles II stated their claim to the grant was invalid.

Initially, North Carolina and South Carolina were one colony; it was known as the Province of Carolina. Carolina is named after King Charles II, even though the first land grant in the Carolina area had been administered by King Charles I.

In 1663, Charles II issued a charter for the land. The Spanish had been making inroads in the region, and Charles II hoped fortifications in the area would put a stop to them. The men who had the charter were known as the Lords Proprietors, with several of these men being involved with the formation and running of other colonies. Although the province had a governor and a council, the Lords Proprietors held the most power. They even controlled who was chosen to be on the council!

The land of the province changed over time, and it was much larger than present-day North and South Carolina today. In 1665, it stretched all the way into Florida. The settlers moved around the land until they found the most suitable areas. This led them to Charleston, which was settled in 1670 as Charles Town. It soon became the seat of government for the province.

Although there was only one seat of government, the northern and southern halves of the province operated independently, for the most part. In 1669, the province was divided into two provinces: Abermarle in the north and Clarendon in the south. In 1691, a governor was appointed to oversee the whole province.

People still referred to the colonies as being separate, though. And eventually, the two would separate. This happened in 1712 after several conflicts, including Cary's Rebellion (an uprising over who would be deputy governor of North Carolina), the Tuscarora War (a war between the Tuscarora, who were upset about the Native American slave trade and the encroaching settlers, and the settlers and their native allies), and the Yamasee War. It was clear to see that the Lords Proprietors were losing their grip on the colonies.

These conflicts all played a major role in the history of the Carolinas, and the two wars deserve a special mention. Due to the Tuscarora War, South Carolina began to better control its slave trade, at least when it came to the Native Americans. The Yamasee War was fought for a number of reasons, of which the slave trade was one. The Native Americans, which included the Yamasee, Cherokee, and Shawnee, just to name a few, devastated South Carolina, killing about 7 percent of its settlers. The Yamasee War was the tipping point that the Carolinas needed to be split into two. It also led to the creation of Georgia, as the Yamasee withdrew from that area after the conflict.

Although South Carolina and North Carolina had two separate governments in 1712, this would not be officially recognized until 1729, which was when the two became royal colonies.

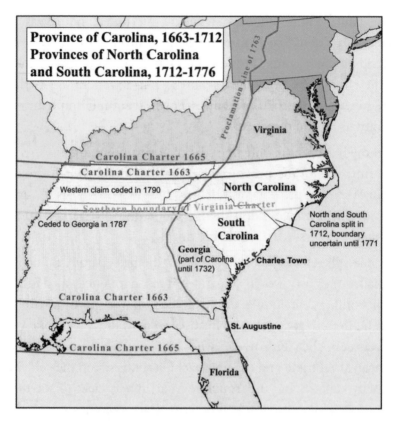

A map of South and North Carolina from 1663 to 1776.

New Netherland

In the early 1600s, the Dutch East India Company set out to explore North America, as it believed a passage existed there that would connect to Asia. Henry Hudson, an English explorer, made inroads in New York for the company, seeking the famous Northwest Passage. He did not find it, but he claimed the lands he discovered for the company. His name might sound familiar to some; Hudson River and Hudson Bay are named after him.

In 1614, New Netherland was established, although it would take some time for the colony to expand and be settled. A year later, the

Dutch would create their first settlement in the Americas: Fort Nassau. This was located near present-day Albany, New York. New Netherland would grow to include parts of New York, New Jersey, and Delaware, just to name a few. Some of the regions it claimed, such as Pennsylvania, were not heavily populated and held only a few outposts.

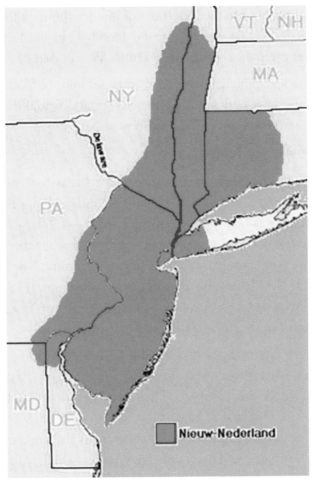

Area settled by the Dutch in the 1660s.

The first Dutch colonists arrived in 1624, and they settled the land and constructed forts. In the 1650s, the Dutch began pushing for even more land, overtaking what was left of New Sweden in 1655. This included Fort Christina, which is now Wilmington, Delaware.

In 1664, the English moved in. Peter Stuyvesant, the director of New Netherland, knew his forces could not face the English without being slaughtered. He ceded the colony to them, although it is important to note that, on paper, the Dutch held the territory until 1674, the year that the Third Anglo-Dutch War ended.

King Charles granted his brother, James, Duke of York, the lands of New Netherland and Maine. New Netherland would then become the Colony of New York and the Colony of New Jersey.

The Colony of New Jersey

James, Duke of York, gave away part of his new territory in late 1664. Sir George Carteret had given the duke help when he was exiled during England's political turmoil in the 1650s when Charles was fighting for his right to the throne after his father died. George's name might sound familiar to some; Carteret County, North Carolina, and Carteret, New Jersey, were both named after him. (He was one of the Lords Proprietors of Carolina.) The other part of New Jersey was sold to a friend of the duke, Lord Berkeley of Stratton.

In 1665, Carteret helped draft the Concession and Agreement, which stated that those who lived in New Jersey could practice whatever religion they wished. They also gave out land to attract settlers, but to obtain this land, they had to pay taxes on it. Many refused to do so, saying their land came from the governor of New York, not New Jersey. To recoup New Jersey's losses, the governor had to sell West Jersey, which the Quakers bought.

Eventually, New Jersey was divided into two: West Jersey and East Jersey. They had their own governors and even their own constitutions. In 1680, Edmund Andros, the governor of New York, sought to control East Jersey, a territory that was overseen by his own cousin. Despite their friendly, familial relationship, Andros had his cousin imprisoned. However, he was unable to gain the territory. This would not be the last time New York and New Jersey jostled over land.

But before getting into the next major conflict between the two territories, we should note that until 1702, New Jersey was a proprietary colony. That changed when the two halves were united. Queen Anne (r. 1702–1707) made it a royal colony, with Edward Hyde becoming the first governor. He was seen as immoral and corrupt. Author Shelly Ross believes that the articles of impeachment in the US Constitution were written due to Hyde's actions. He allegedly liked to cross-dress, which would have been scandalous back then (so scandalous, in fact, that it seems very unlikely that he would have done so in public as some state). There are firsthand accounts of him opening the New York Assembly while dressed as a woman, but historians today contend that it is possible these writers were trying to assassinate his character. Hyde also accepted bribes, embezzled, and poorly managed funds, just to name a few. No one seemed to care for him, and no one seemed to be upset when he was recalled to England in 1708. Well, perhaps they were a little upset. Once Hyde left, New Jersey was overseen by the governor of New York. In 1738, a separate governor for New Jersey was installed.

While these events were going on, New Jersey and New York were poking at each other in the New York-New Jersey Line War (1701–1765). Many colonies engaged in border wars, but this is thought to be the largest one; around 210,000 acres were at stake. In the end, the border was established at the confluence of the Delaware and Neversink Rivers.

The Colony of New York

New York's beginning sounds a lot like New Jersey's. In 1664, James, Duke of York, was given New Netherland, of which New York was a part. Unlike New Jersey, though, James did not sell New York.

So, when he took the throne in 1685, James II's territory became a royal colony.

James II would be removed from the throne in 1688 due to the Glorious Revolution, which saw his daughter, Mary II, and her husband, William of Orange, take the throne. Again, the internal conflicts in England could be felt in the Americas. At the time, Edmund Andros was serving as the governor of the Dominion of New England, a short-lived government venture. This will be talked about more in a future chapter, but to briefly summarize, the Dominion oversaw a large portion of New England, including New York and New Jersey, which means these colonies no longer had their own governor.

Edmund Andros was overthrown, and New York began its process to restore its former government, something that was seen throughout all of the former Dominion of New England. Francis Nicholson, a captain in the English navy who had served as the lieutenant governor of the Dominion, took charge of New York. In the summer of 1689, he headed to England, and Jacob Leisler, a German-born merchant, took the opportunity and installed himself as the leader of the southern part of New York. He collected taxes and even attempted to take control of parts of Canada. In 1691, the royally appointed governor, Henry Sloughter, arrived. He had Leisler arrested, and he was later tried and executed.

The Colony of Pennsylvania

In 1681, Pennsylvania received its official charter. It was granted to William Penn by Charles II, who was restored to the throne on May 29th, 1660. Penn, a writer and a firm believer in Quakerism, sought to establish a space for Quakers.

As a Quaker, William Penn faced jail time for not shying away from his religious beliefs. In his writings, he criticized Catholics, Anglicans, and others. He wrote *No Cross, No Crown*, one of his most important works, while in jail. Penn gained influence in legal matters too. He helped free Quakers and political prisoners from prison.

Penn maintained a friendship with Charles II and his brother, James, Duke of York. In 1681, Penn, along with eleven other Quakers, bought the rights to the eastern side of New Jersey. Afterward, he received present-day Delaware from the duke of York. Despite this, Penn sought to buy the land from the Lenape, who already lived on the land.

William Penn used the opportunity to design laws based on the Quaker mindset. Residents received the freedom to practice their religion, and all Christians were welcome. Plus, their rights as Englishmen remained protected. In addition, Penn influenced the beginnings of Philadelphia, which was founded in 1682 and served as the seat of the province's government. A more complete history of colonial Pennsylvania can be found in Chapter 5.

The Colony of Georgia

Georgia was the last of the Thirteen Colonies to be established. It was first established in 1732, but it would receive royal status in 1752. In many ways, it was a special colony. King George II was involved in its establishment, as he signed the charter for it, and it was named after him. James Oglethorpe, who served as a minister in British Parliament, was granted authority over the project. He would be the governor of Georgia for over a decade.

George II's rule is notable for several reasons, including the Seven Years' War against France. When he passed away, his grandson, George III, took the throne. He had to deal with the tail end of that very same war, which manifested on the North American continent as the French and Indian War.

After James Oglethorpe secured the charter for Georgia, he aimed to turn it into a colony that gave individuals a second chance. He spent time in London helping individuals who could not pay off their debts, and he also worked with the poor. Once a person fell into debt in Britain, there was not much they could do to gain their position back. Given that the economy experienced severe fluctuations, there was no real way out of poverty for most individuals. Oglethorpe came up with the idea of shipping these two groups of people to the New World to give them a new start.

He led a crew of over one hundred settlers to the New World, landing in what is now Savannah. None of the trustees received land from the charter. Georgia was set up more as a charity, not for making a profit. The Georgia trustees saw how South Carolina had developed. The colony contained large tracts of land and many indentured servants and African slaves. Therefore, the Georgia trustees placed a size limit on the parcels of land.

The trustees also kept the colony's leadership to themselves. They did not establish a representative assembly. The goal was to achieve social control. In the leaders' eyes, the people who were shipped to Georgia were poor, and there was no way to know if they had the capacity to govern themselves. After all, many had already gotten themselves into trouble with debt.

History tells that the proprietors used a lot of idealism to establish the colony. They outlawed slavery and heavy drinking, and they also granted religious freedom. Georgia had fertile land, but without the extra labor, it was difficult to churn out enough products to meet demand in those early days when the population was low.

Oglethorpe's time in office ended in 1743, and the trustees began to lose interest in the colony. The colony started to see changes as a result. In 1749, it was decided that the ban on slavery would be lifted. The economy also remained weak, and Georgia placed a focus on exporting lumber. To pick things up economically, Georgia started to resemble South Carolina. Otherwise, it would require constant subsidies. African slaves did make their way to Georgia eventually, but the colony did not become exactly like South Carolina. There was variation within the population. By the time Georgia became a state, it had the most plantations. This was probably a result of the land limits being removed.

In the mid-1700s, many Spanish still resided in Florida. Their closeness to the settlers in Georgia led to renewed tensions between the two powers. The Georgia settlers, with Oglethorpe's leadership, successfully established the border between the two territories.

In 1755, Georgia was no longer a proprietary colony; instead, it became a royal colony.

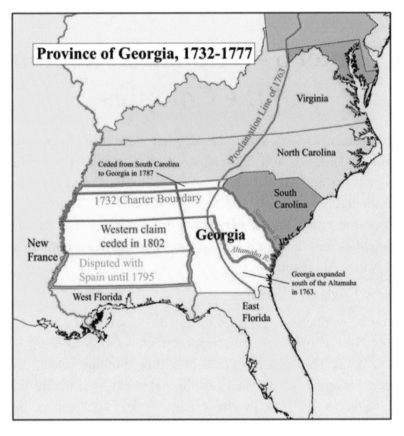

Map of Colony of Georgia.

Chapter 3 – The Three Regions of the Colonies

The Thirteen Colonies can be divided into three regions: New England, Middle, and Southern. Each region had different demographics and natural resources to utilize. Each settlement had to build shelter, procure food, and clothe its people, but as time went on, this became easier and easier to do. In the beginning, the settlers would either find their path on their own and/or depend on assistance from Native Americans.

New England Colonies

The New England Colonies included Massachusetts Bay, Rhode Island, New Hampshire, and Connecticut, as well as some other smaller ones. This area was great for fishing, hunting, and procuring lumber. However, it consisted of hills and rocky soil, which made it challenging to grow crops on a large scale. The settlers in this northernmost region of the Thirteen Colonies did grow things, though, such as squash, beans, and corn.

When the colonists first arrived in the region in the early 1600s, there were many Native American tribes already living there, such as the Wampanoag, Pequot, and Narragansett, just to name a few.

Although the natives and the colonists traded with each other and even assisted one another, there were a lot of conflicts. The tensions between the Europeans and Native Americans tended to develop over time. In the mid- to late 1600s, wars broke out, such as the Pequot War (1636–1638) and King Philip's War (1675–1678). Both wars were deadly, with the Pequots being wiped out nearly to extinction. And while King Philip's War saw many Wampanoag and other natives killed or enslaved, the European population of Plymouth and Rhode Island was decimated. It is believed they lost one-tenth of their fighting men.

Many people know of the horrors Africans faced in the colonies, but some may be unaware of the enslavement of Native Americans. Many Native American slaves were sold to plantations in the West Indies, where the conditions were notoriously difficult and harsh. And while some people might point out that Native Americans kept slaves themselves, their form of slavery tended to be less oppressive.

Speaking of slavery, New York had an astounding number of slaves. By 1703, over 42 percent of New York homes had slaves, putting New York behind only Charleston, South Carolina, in regards to the slave population.

Middle Colonies

New York was not a part of the New England Colonies; it belonged to the Middle Colonies. The Middle Colonies also included Delaware, New Jersey, and Pennsylvania.

Where the Middle Colonies were located.

These colonies had more fertile soil than the New England Colonies, which tended to be rockier. The Middle Colonies grew and exported many grains, such as hemp, wheat, and flax. They exported so many grains that it became known as the Breadbasket Colonies. In addition to this, the region was heavily forested, leading to the establishment of the lumber industry. Pennsylvania was successful in the textile and iron industries as well.

Before the colonists arrived, the region was inhabited by Native American tribes, including but not limited to the Mohawks, Lenape, and Mohicans. The colonies embraced diversity, and there were times when peace with Native Americans was the norm.

Due to this diversity, which included not only different ethnicities (such as Scottish, Irish, German, English, French, Dutch, etc.) but also different religions (such as Methodism, Quakerism, Calvinism, Lutheranism, etc.), the Middle Colonies tended to be more socially tolerant. This was very different than the New England Colonies, where Puritanism tended to reign supreme. In the Middle Colonies, though, immigrants were welcomed with open arms, although part of this might be due to the fact that these colonies had a hard time keeping up with demand.

Indentured servitude was common. Men, women, and sometimes even teenagers wanted to make their way to the New World but had no money. A deal would be struck where they would be provided free passage in return for working on a farm or learning a trade for a certain number of years. They would work off their debt, meaning they would be free after it had been worked off. Between the 1630s and the 1790s, it is believed that around one-half to two-thirds of European immigrants came to the colonies as indentured servants.

Slavery did exist, which is apparent by the high number of African slaves in New York. The major cities tended to depend on slave labor more, and they were usually used as domestic slaves. The Middle Colonies didn't rely on slaves for their economy as much as the Southern Colonies did, though.

Southern Colonies

The Southern Colonies consisted of Virginia, North and South Carolina, Georgia, and Maryland. It would eventually grow to include the colonies of Florida, but the United States held them for only around twenty years (1763–1783), so their history is not touched on much in this book. The Spanish maintained control over Florida for most of colonial America. Today, Florida is a part of the United States; it was finally gained in 1819 due to the Adams-Onis Treaty.

The Southern Colonies had incredibly fertile soil, access to waterways, and a warm, agreeable climate most of the year. Even their winters were (and still are) fairly mild. It is no surprise that these colonies produced most of the crops that were exported. They grew many things, but the most profitable were tobacco, rice, and indigo. Cotton was grown, but it would not become an important crop until the invention of the cotton gin in 1793. Fewer people inhabited the towns in the Southern Colonies in comparison to New England because the bulk of the land was used to grow crops.

Native Americans, such as the Powhatan, Cherokee, and Tuscarora, just to name a few, called these colonies home long before the colonists arrived. The settlers' initial interactions with the natives were, for the most part, peaceful. But like in the other colonies, these interactions tended to turn violent over time. Colonists in all three regions continued encroaching on the natives' land and ignoring promises that had been made. In addition, the colonists sought to "civilize" the Native Americans by imposing their religion and customs on them. Interactions with the Europeans benefited the Native Americans to an extent, but it also saw the deterioration of their own cultures in the process. Unfortunately, due to the European mindset back then, this outcome was likely inevitable for the Native Americans, and it remains a tragic part of United States history.

Another tragic part of US history is, of course, slavery. And the Southern Colonies utilized this practice the most of the three major regions. It took time for slavery to take hold, as many people started out at the bottom and had to work their way to the top. The cash crops of tobacco, indigo, and rice began to be highly demanded, but these crops are labor-intensive to plant, grow, and harvest. To keep up with demand, the colonists turned to the African slave trade. The Africans, similar to the Native Americans, were seen as "lesser." More often than not, their lives were incredibly hard, with punishing hours and even more punishing masters.

The Southern Colonies began to rely so heavily on slavery that the people could see no other way to keep the economy afloat. Today, people think of large plantations with many slaves as being the norm, but that was not the case. The South consisted of many small farms, which would typically have at least one slave. This changed over time, though, as most things do. By the time of the Civil War (1861–1865), buying a slave was incredibly expensive due to the more restrictive slavery laws, so smaller farms often did not have slaves unless they had been inherited or gifted.

Since the Southern Colonies had so many individuals working as slaves, they outnumbered the non-labor (really, the white) population. Due to this, there was a great fear of revolts breaking out. In 1739, their worst fear did take place. This was a slave revolt in South Carolina known as the Stono Rebellion or Cato's Rebellion.

In early September, a slave named Cato led a group of slaves to Spanish Florida in hopes they could live in freedom. On the first day of the revolt, they stormed down the street, killed two shopkeepers, and raided their stores. On their way to Florida, they gathered slaves; it is believed they gathered around eighty of them. They also burned plantations and killed around thirty European colonists.

However, the residents of South Carolina did fight back. They managed to catch up to the slaves, and in the confrontation, around twenty colonists and nearly fifty slaves were killed. The ones who survived continued to flee toward Florida, but they were tracked down. Most of them were executed, while the others were sold to the West Indies, which was deemed to be one of the worst places to be enslaved due to the terrible working conditions and hot environment.

This rebellion led to the Negro Act of 1740. To ensure rebellions would not be commonplace, plantations had to maintain a ratio of one white to every ten Africans. Slaves could not grow their own food, assemble in groups, earn money, or learn to read. It also ensured that slaves would not be brutally punished by imposing penalties on those colonists who engaged in such behavior. Of course, this still happened. Few cared if such things happened, and on top of that, slaves could not testify against a white person.

South Carolina was the largest importer of slaves in North America, with over fifty-eight thousand Africans entering the colony between 1750 and 1775. Almost all of the slaves that came to the New World passed through Charleston (Charles Town) first. During the colonial period, the transatlantic slave trade ensured that slaves continued to arrive on the shores of the Southern Colonies. Traders would bring Africans over on large ships, where they were subjected to terrible conditions. Between 1500 and 1866, it is estimated that nearly two million out of 12.5 million slaves were killed on the long voyage. Not all of these slaves went to what would become the United States, though. In comparison to other areas, the intake of slaves was rather minor. According to Henry Louis Gates, Jr., the director of the Hutchins Center for African and African American research, around 388,000 of the 12.5 million slaves who came to the New World went to North America. Most slaves that came to the New World went to the Caribbean and South America. However, the trade would continue until 1808 when it was banned, and it continued on after that, albeit illegally.

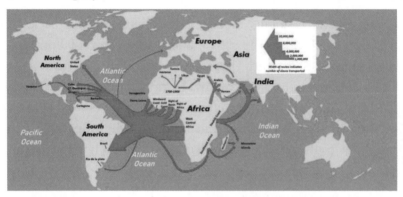

Slave trade between 1500 and 1900.

The slave trade played a key role in what was included in the Declaration of Independence, a document that was written in 1776 to declare the colonists' independence from Great Britain. Thomas Jefferson, who was the primary author of it, condemned the practice of slavery in an early draft. Although he owned slaves himself (it is estimated he owned more than six hundred throughout his life), he saw the institution as being evil, foisting most of the blame on King George III. Jefferson wrote, "He [King George] has waged cruel war against human nature itself, violating its most sacred rights of life & liberty in the persons of a distant people who never offended him, captivating & carrying them into slavery in another hemisphere or to incur miserable death in their transportation thither."

Jefferson stopped short of calling for the ban of slavery altogether (though he would later put together such a plan in the early 1800s), but even so, this passage was stripped from the Declaration of Independence. One-third of the signers had a vested interest in the practice, and alienating them would be too hard of a blow.

The issue of slavery was still debated during the American Revolution and afterward, but the institution was left intact to please the Southern Colonies, with more restrictions being placed on the practice over the years. Slavery in the United States would only end after the Civil War in 1865.

Chapter 4 – A Closer Look: Massachusetts

Colonial Massachusetts played a large role in the founding of the United States of America, so it bears a closer look. As the largest colony in the New England area, it indirectly helped found Rhode Island and Connecticut. Boston was also one of the most important colonial cities. It became a center for trade, innovation, and politics.

The first colonial college was established in Massachusetts; this was none other than Harvard, and it was established in 1636. In those days, colleges educated clergy. Thus, the colonial colleges had a denomination. For Harvard, it was Congregational. Congregationalists, a Protestant denomination, believe that each congregation should be run autonomously, not by a higher church official.

Massachusetts Bay Colony was not the first colony the English established in the New World, but it was certainly the most prosperous of the New England Colonies.

Its beginnings go back to the Pilgrims. These were Separatists who were seeking a different way to worship their religion. They disagreed with the Church of England and its mandates. The Separatists first made their way to Holland in 1608, where they were allowed to worship and flourish. As their families grew, they worried about the Dutch influence on their children. Even though they had fled England, they wanted to remain Englishmen and women. Thus, they wanted to raise their children in that culture too.

From their base in Holland, the Separatists negotiated with the Virginia Company. They intended to land near the Hudson River, which at that time was considered to be part of northern Virginia. After some setbacks and delays, 102 men, women, and children boarded the *Mayflower* in 1620. It set sail and spent sixty-six days at sea. The winds veered them away from their intended settlement, instead sailing the ship toward Cape Cod, which is located in modern-day southeastern Massachusetts.

The Embarkation of the Pilgrims *(1857) by Robert Walter Weir.*

https://commons.wikimedia.org/wiki/File:Embarkation_of_the_Pilgrims.jpg

Once they found a shoreline on which to land, they didn't deboard immediately. They wanted to find the Hudson River, which was where they were supposed to settle. While they sailed about looking for a good place to call their own, the passengers acknowledged that there was no charter ruling over them or the way they were going to live. As a result, the leadership put together the Mayflower Compact.

The Mayflower Compact was one of the earliest governing documents in what would become the United States. Other colonies would follow its example.

After sixty-six days at sea, tensions were high among the passengers. Not everyone on board was a Separatist. When those who had different views than the Pilgrims realized that they were outside the jurisdiction of their destination, it caused some chaos. Since the people were no longer bound to a charter due to the fact they were not landing in Virginia, they wanted to leave the group and settle on their own. Although they may not have realized it on the *Mayflower*, they needed each other. The numbers were not on their side.

The Mayflower Compact was only around two hundred words long. William Bradford and William Brewster, men who would play an integral role in the shaping of Plymouth Colony, helped draft it. The document established a government that bound each of the members on board the ship. To keep the group afloat, they agreed that laws and regulations for the good of the colony applied to each member. It was a voluntary way to self-govern. Forty-one adult male passengers signed it.

William Bradford was the governor of Plymouth Colony for a combined total of about thirty years. During his time in office (and even while not in office), he had great influence over the shaping of the colony. Bradford was part of a Separatist group that traveled to Holland in 1609. When the economic opportunities for the Separatists began to wane, he helped organize the expedition from Holland to the New World that set sail in 1620.

Thanks to Bradford, the colony got off to a good start. He helped establish the principles of self-governance. Impressively, he also set down guidelines that helped nonbelievers assimilate to the colony's culture.

William Brewster helped lead the Separatist migration from England to Amsterdam. He maintained a leadership role during their time in Holland. Brewster printed Puritan books that the English government had banned. The English authorities found out in 1619 and seized them. Brewster managed to escape before they could arrest him, and he became part of the Virginia Company. Brewster sailed on the *Mayflower* with the Pilgrims in 1620. Thanks to his education, he became the senior elder of the church, and he helped shape its customs.

The passengers would eventually land in what is now Plymouth, Massachusetts. Funding for the *Mayflower's* voyage came from John Carver, who was a deacon in the Netherlands. After the formation of Plymouth Colony, he was elected as its first governor. Carver also managed to strike peace between Wampanoag Chief Massasoit in 1621, with their treaty lasting for over fifty years.

New England winters were (and still remain) harsh. Americans had to learn how to survive them as they established their infrastructure, which was made easier after formal contact with the local tribes. The Pilgrims weren't prepared for the elements, especially that first winter. Only 44 of the original 102 survived. As they got hold of their bearings, they learned how to find, pick, and store food, with their techniques being greatly enhanced by the Native Americans, namely Squanto.

The Massachusetts Bay Colony charter was issued in 1629, establishing the colony as a charter colony. A fleet of ships carrying over seven hundred settlers set off for the colony in 1630. This was just one of the many voyages that took place during what is known as the Great Puritan Migration. Several more fleets followed, with most of them arriving by 1640. Although Puritans came after 1640, the number of those who dared to cross the ocean greatly dwindled. They headed for Massachusetts, as well as to modern-day Maine, New Hampshire, Rhode Island, Connecticut, Virginia, and Maryland. Puritans also headed toward the Caribbean islands, such as Barbados and St. Kitts.

In Massachusetts, John Winthrop, the leader of the fleet in 1630, became one of the notable heads of the colony. Although Winthrop led a life according to Puritan values, he had enjoyed a good life in England. On his voyage to Massachusetts, he composed a sermon called "A Model of Christian Charity," which he delivered aboard the *Arbella* on April 8th, 1630.

In 1629, Winthrop was voted as the governor of the new colony; this was before he even set sail for the New World. Also, in 1629, Winthrop and Thomas Dudley, among others, signed the Cambridge Agreement in August 1629. Essentially, it stipulated that those who went to the New World could buy shares from shareholders who stayed behind in England. It also stated that Massachusetts Bay Colony would be ruled by a local power in New England instead of being controlled by the shareholders in the Old World. Dudley served as a deputy governor and governor for a total of seventeen years. He contributed as a civil servant and was a leader in education. Dudley helped establish Roxbury Latin School, and he signed Harvard's new charter in 1650. His daughter, Anne Bradstreet, was one of the earliest American poets.

Although Dudley made important contributions to the colony, they are often overshadowed by Winthrop, who was quite popular among the freemen of Massachusetts. Winthrop served as governor from 1631 to 1649, off and on. All the colonies and colonial territories found ways to govern themselves since they were so far from England. In Massachusetts, only members of the Congregational church received the right to vote. The irony is that under this system, more men received a voice than they did in England. Property owners also received a voice in town affairs.

Since Winthrop ruled with an iron fist, his popularity waned, although he always remained somewhat beloved. During his time in charge, opposition grew toward Puritanism. Individuals, such as Roger Williams and Anne Hutchinson, had different ideas about how people should relate to God. Winthrop led the charge against Anne

Hutchinson. Somehow, she managed to take a leadership role in the community in regard to religion. She hosted local meetings, inviting men and women to discuss sermons, something that was discouraged back then. A minister's sermon was to be taken at face value, not debated about behind closed doors.

After becoming mired in the Antinomian controversy, Hutchinson was accused of heresy. Put very simply, Anne Hutchinson was a free grace advocate. She believed that people do not have to do good works to attain salvation; rather, good works were a part of being a Christian. Eternal life was free to any who believed. These ideas were heretical at the time, especially in Puritan-controlled Massachusetts. Anne Hutchinson was excommunicated from the colony in 1638.

A drawing of Anne Hutchinson on trial by Edwin Austin Abbey.

https://en.wikipedia.org/wiki/File:Anne_Hutchinson_on_Trial.jpg

Another prominent figure in early colonial Massachusetts was John Cotton. Cotton fled England due to the persecution of his non-conforming beliefs. He was an avid Puritan. He became embroiled in controversy in the New World as well since he encouraged Anne Hutchinson's beliefs. However, during her trial, he had to reprimand her for not conducting herself properly. Back then, the colonies did not practice democracy. Men like Winthrop and Cotton believed that laws were meant to enforce God's will and religious rules.

John Endecott held these same beliefs as well, and no chapter on Massachusetts history would be complete without at least mentioning him. He is thought to be one of the Fathers of New England, and he was the longest-serving governor of Massachusetts Bay Colony. He was a firm believer in Puritanism, but he also firmly believed in Separatism, which was not a popular belief among the Puritans. Regardless, Endecott did not think men should be able to make decisions if they did not have Puritan interests at heart.

Increase Mather and his son, Cotton Mather, also played an important role in religious affairs. Both father and son were Puritan clergymen, and they both played an important role in the Salem witch trials. Between February 1692 and May 1693, more than two hundred people, both men and women, were accused of witchcraft. In Salem Village (present-day Danvers, Massachusetts), the daughter and niece of Samuel Parris, the reverend, began to have fits. In time, the number of those afflicted grew.

The girls accused three women of causing their odd behavior. One of these women, Tituba, was a slave, and she corroborated what the young girls were saying, that someone had put an enchantment on them. She even said that there were more witches living among them. The two other women, Sarah Good and Sarah Osborn, were likely targeted because of their oddities. Good was homeless, and Osborn was incredibly reclusive. In other words, all three women were seen as outcasts.

Hysteria swept the town and the neighboring villages. Upstanding citizens started to be accused, which led to even more paranoia. If people who bettered the community could be witches, then anyone could be one.

Of course, it is highly unlikely that there were actually witches. It is not known what exactly caused the trials to occur, but it is likely a combination of factors, such as family feuds, bored/hysterical children, and politics within the church. Some scholars have even proposed that the teenage girls ate moldy bread, which caused hallucinations, and that mass panic set in once people started taking the accusations seriously.

The people who were accused were put under tremendous pressure to confess. And this is meant literally. Giles Corey was pressed to death for his refusal to plead guilty. In total, nineteen people were hung for the crime of witchcraft, with at least five other people dying in jail.

Cotton Mather and Increase Mather believed in witchcraft, but they also believed that the people deserved a fair trial. Spectral evidence had been allowed in court proceedings. A person was allowed to say that they saw the apparition of the person afflicting them. Some believed that the Devil needed a person's permission to use their visage, which is why the court allowed this kind of evidence. Almost all of the evidence submitted in court was spectral evidence, which is not surprising, considering how hard it was to disprove. Cotton Mather even said, "Do not lay more stress on pure spectral evidence than it will bear...It is very certain that the Devils have sometimes represented the shapes of persons not only innocent, but also very virtuous." Increase Mather shared the same beliefs, saying, "It would better that ten suspected witches may escape than one innocent person be condemned." This kind of evidence was allowed until October 1692.

The Salem witch trials are still remembered today as a dark period of US history. However, there were many positives, especially in Massachusetts Bay Colony. In terms of the colony's economy, John Winthrop the Younger (the son of John Winthrop) established the Saugus Works in 1644. The system had a dam that provided water. It connected to a smelting furnace, forge, and rolling mill, complete with a slitter. It had the capability to produce two types of iron: pourable and pig. This is described as the beginning of the colonial iron industry. The Saugus Works helped spawn an estimated 175 more plants across the colonies. Since England made great use of the products these ironworks churned out, they eliminated custom duties on it.

For the most part, in the early days of the colony, Massachusetts lived in relative peace. The majority of the freemen retained similar values, and there were no major issues to disagree on until people like Anne Hutchinson and Roger Williams began popping up. Tensions rose even more when the Quakers started showing up in 1656. The Quakers also ventured to the new land from England. Since their religious views differed from the Puritans, they rocked the boat. To keep the peace, the leadership banished the Quakers, Anabaptists, and individuals like Roger Williams and Anne Hutchinson.

The residents of Massachusetts had their rebellious side, though, and England recognized it. The colony's charter was revoked in 1684 for several reasons. Violations included trading with other countries; the Navigation Acts, which were instituted throughout the 1600s, prevented this. The colony was also caught melting English coins to create their own money that did not have the image of the king on them. Perhaps most damning, the residents of Massachusetts Bay Colony created laws that did not fit with what was established in England, particularly laws based on religion.

England spent a good amount of time and funds keeping the colonies in line. In 1686, the royal authority created the Dominion of New England to enforce the Navigation Acts. These acts helped bolster England's shipping, trade, and fleets, and they restricted the colonies from depending on other foreign goods. As the colonies developed their own economies and trading abilities, they started trading with countries outside of England's circle. England had to put a stop to that, as the wars it participated in against the other European powers greatly drained its coffers. And at the end of the day, the colonies belonged to England to serve the Crown. Any goods they produced needed to benefit England first.

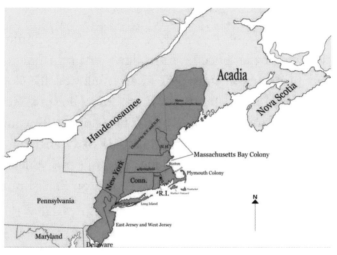

A map of the Dominion of New England, 1688.

Tpwissaa, CC BY-SA 4.0 <https://creativecommons.org/licenses/by-sa/4.0>, via Wikimedia Commons https://commons.wikimedia.org/wiki/File:NE_Dominion.png

The Dominion set up shop in Boston, Massachusetts. The Dominion got off to a rocky start, with the local officials refusing to acknowledge it. In late 1686, Sir Edmund Andros, the governor of New York, took control of the Dominion. He was pro-Church of England while Boston remained set in its puritanical ways. He made it clear that the colonists had no rights as Englishmen since they did not live in England. Laws were made that aligned more closely with that of England's, but Andros had a hard time getting the colonists to follow them. Landowners needed to receive land patents, and local taxes rose. The soldiers who accompanied Andros were far from saints too, which only exacerbated tensions.

In essence, Andros made attempts to quench the colonists' thirst for independence. In some ways, the Dominion of New England foreshadowed what was to come in the 1760s. The Declaration of Independence and the United States Constitution stem from English culture and laws. When Britain felt like it was losing its grip on the colonies, it tightened its grip on them. For instance, Andros began canceling town meetings, placing restrictions on the courts, and revoking land titles. Restrictions on the press and schools were also put into place.

During Andros's time serving as governor of the Dominion, the British Crown experienced instability. Every time England experienced problems at the royal level, it allowed the colonies to breathe easier again. In this case, it was the Glorious Revolution, which took place from 1688 to 1689. The Glorious Revolution saw James II, a Catholic, dethroned. William III of Orange and James's daughter, Mary II, became the king and queen. William was a Protestant Dutchman, while Mary was an Anglican Englishwoman.

The change in power caused the Dominion of New England to tumble. Once the colonists found out, it gave them the confidence to rebel. They reasserted their power in their respective colonies. Andros attempted to flee, but the colonists caught him, along with the other leaders sent by the Crown. They were held in captivity for ten months with no trial before being put on a ship back to England.

When the Dominion dissolved, Massachusetts and Plymouth Colony were in a weird spot. If you can recall, Plymouth never had an official royal charter, and Massachusetts had lost theirs. Without a charter, there was no reason for these colonies to even exist. The leaders of Massachusetts worked hard, and in 1691, the charter was restored, but it was far from the original. It also established that Plymouth and parts of the Province of New York would become part of the colony.

The new charter caused chaos for the Puritans. It did away with tying voting rights to church membership. Massachusetts's new royal status delivered a new royal governor. The colonists no longer filled the positions of authority; British appointees filled them instead.

The colonies became important for England, especially during the many conflicts that England was facing. They provided England with lumber, tobacco, and dried fish, among many other things. Trade with Britain, in turn, gave the colonies manufactured goods and textiles.

Massachusetts Bay Colony started as an agricultural economy. Farmers grew corn and raised cattle. Keep in mind that the colonists learned a lot through trial and error. As the population of Massachusetts grew, they overused the soil. When they realized that the soil was depleted of its nutrients, they had to find other ways to keep the economy alive. Their proximity to the Atlantic Ocean meant that they had access to maritime activities, so they balanced their economy with fishing. Their access to timber allowed them to build fishing vessels. In turn, this gave birth to merchants, tradesmen, and craftsmen.

Massachusetts continued to flourish, even after the American Revolution. The colony played an important role in the war, as it became the site of the first military engagements of the revolution: the Battles of Lexington and Concord.

Chapter 5 – A Closer Look: Pennsylvania

The famous Quaker William Penn named Philadelphia, one of the most influential cities of colonial America, in Pennsylvania. Philadelphia is the combination of two Greek words: *phileo* and *adelphos*, or "beloved" and "brother." That's why Philadelphia is known as the City of Brotherly Love.

Although Penn was a student at the University of Oxford, he rejected the Anglican teachings. In 1662, he was expelled for nonconformity. Two years later, Penn came across Thomas Loe, a Quaker missionary, for the second time in his life. This time, Penn made his membership in the Society of Friends permanent.

Penn left behind many books, treatises, and pamphlets. When he received an opportunity to preach his Quaker principles to a group of people, he did. Penn's nonconformity got him in trouble on several occasions. In 1668, he was imprisoned for his beliefs. Two years later, England banned religious public meetings of more than five people. Penn and his friend William Mead ignored this and were arrested for preaching at a Quaker meetinghouse in London. During his trial, Penn showed his ability to defend himself. He asked for a copy of the charges that were being levied against him, but the judge refused. On top of this, the judge wouldn't let the defense present their case. The jury found Penn not guilty, and they were punished for it. They were imprisoned and fined.

Jury tampering was commonplace at this time. The Crown and its representatives expected to receive their desired verdict every time. Sometimes they rigged the juries. Other times, the juries experienced threats to coerce them into giving the proper verdict.

As time passes, it's easy to forget why the Founding Fathers integrated the Bill of Rights. Today, Americans expect to receive a fair trial and a jury of their peers. In colonial America, this was often not the case. Today, American citizens also receive the right against unlawful searches and seizures.

Back in Penn's time, though, the jury should have acquiesced to the judge. However, they refused and filed what is known as Bushel's Case. The case established that juries could not be punished for not delivering a certain verdict, although jury members could be fined or imprisoned if they behaved inappropriately.

Many of the most famous American colonial historical figures maintained journals. Without their writings, American history would be a guessing game. Penn's day in court was published in *The People's Ancient and Just Liberties Asserted* in 1670.

When Penn's father, an admiral and politician, passed away in 1670, he inherited the estates. In 1671 and 1677, Penn undertook missions to Holland and Germany. There, he made contact with people who would help him populate Pennsylvania.

The year 1681 began Penn's journey toward proprietorship. With eleven Quakers, he purchased the rights to East New Jersey from Sir George Carteret's heirs. Penn put together the pieces of the land, and he named the colony after his father. Charles II got the ball rolling, but the duke of York granted Penn the Lower Counties, which today make up Delaware.

The Birth of Pennsylvania *(1680) by Jean Leon Gerome Ferris.*

Penn saw the colony as a religious experiment. He assembled the Frame of Government, with his goal being to write a set of rules that would prevent future leaders from "doing mischief" with their power. Penn integrated his Quaker and Whig ideas into the framework. Whigs did not believe in an absolute monarchy; rather, they wanted a constitutional monarchy.

The first city that Penn's crew assembled was Philadelphia. Penn asked them to lay it out in a grid pattern. The pattern made it easy to hand out parcels of land. In time, Pennsylvania became the largest shipbuilding colony. Thanks to the colony's success, it attracted notable men, such as Benjamin Franklin. Franklin was born in Boston, but he spent so much time in Philadelphia that the people claim him as his own.

Franklin moved there at the tender age of seventeen. A few years later, in 1729, he started publishing *The Pennsylvania Gazette.* In 1731, Franklin founded the Library Company of Philadelphia. This library continues to collect important historical documents that tell the story of America. The library has also become a research center. It boasts a collection of 500,000 books. The collection includes rare books, prints, photographs, manuscripts, and pamphlets. It makes sense that the library collects so many printed items; after all, Franklin championed the printing press in Philadelphia.

Promoting the written word was just one of Franklin's many accomplishments. During the colonial period, fires threatened homes, as open fires were common in colonial America. The colonists used them for warming their homes during the winter and for burning trash. In Philadelphia, fires were a particular problem. In 1736, Benjamin Franklin established the first volunteer fire department in colonial America. Groups of thirty men put out fires, and they also met regularly to discuss issues impacting their area. The fire department led to the establishment of the first insurance company in the United States.

By 1770, Philadelphia grew to hold a population of around thirty thousand. This is quite impressive, as only twenty years before, the population was twenty-five thousand. In 1776, the population of the Thirteen Colonies reached 2.5 million. The largest city was Philadelphia, with forty thousand people. New York, Boston, and Charleston followed with twenty-five thousand, fifteen thousand, and twelve thousand, respectively. Although the first official census didn't take place until 1790, these estimates are thought to be close.

These population numbers include slaves. Since the inhabitants of Pennsylvania were mostly Quakers, they had to reconcile several realities in regards to slavery. Some of the original inhabitants, including William Penn, tolerated the act. Slavery was already present in the region by the time they arrived, as the Dutch and Swedes brought slaves with them and/or bought them after becoming established. However, as time passed, many Quakers did their best to protest the act. The 1688 Germantown Petition Against Slavery was the first protest against slavery in the New World. The petition placed emphasis on the Golden Rule ("Do unto others as you would have them do unto you").

Francis Daniel Pastorius drafted the petition with three local Quakers. Pastorius helped found Germantown in Pennsylvania. He was of German descent, and he was an author, humanitarian, and educator. The German Quakers signed him as an agent of the Frankfurt Land Company in 1683. Right off the bat, he purchased fifteen thousand acres from Penn. This became Germantown. In 1707, Germantown lost its charter. It would become a part of Philadelphia in 1854.

Historians haven't decided if the four men who drafted the petition expected any real action. They knew that abolishing slavery in the whole colony would have been almost impossible. However, the document played an important role in the abolition movement in the mid-1800s. Its wording likely influenced the Declaration of Independence, which sought to create fairness for all men (although it should be noted that this wasn't necessarily the case).

Pennsylvania didn't have a great need for slaves. Their economy consisted of exporting and importing iron goods. The colony had access to iron ore, and they produced tools, plows, nails, and kettles. Pennsylvania had an agricultural economy as well, producing crops like wheat and corn. The people raised livestock, which means they had access to dairy products. In addition to manufacturing iron goods, the residents of Pennsylvania also produced paper goods and textiles. Their proximity to bodies of water helped them become worthy shipbuilders too.

Chapter 6 – A Closer Look: Virginia

Although Jamestown was the first permanent English settlement in what would become the United States, it almost didn't turn out that way. The Virginia Company of London received its charter in 1606 and founded the settlement a year later. However, due to the colonists' late arrival, they were unable to plant crops. It also didn't help that many who went on the voyage were not used to hard labor. Before ships arrived in 1608 to aid in the relief effort, two-thirds of the settlers had died. More people were brought on these relief ships, exacerbating the issues the colony was already facing. In addition to this, the investors of the Virginia Company were unhappy with the profits. The task to turn the colony around fell on Captain John Smith.

A lot of lore surrounds Captain John Smith. The captain was undoubtedly an adventurer, soldier, and explorer. He was also an author. His family rented a farm from a local lord, and he was able to attend school, where he learned how to read, write, and do arithmetic. Legend has it that he ran away from home at the age of thirteen. He wanted to become a sailor; however, his father found him before he got too far.

When Smith's father passed away in 1596, he left home. In 1598, he became a mercenary for the French, who were fighting against the Spanish in the Netherlands. The experience helped sow the seeds for his fighting and exploring tendencies. Supposedly, Smith even killed three Ottomans in duels. He also managed to escape enslavement by beguiling his mistress. His life is filled with other legendary exploits, so it is hard to know what is fact and what is fiction.

In 1606, Smith became involved with the Virginia Company's venture. However, on his way to the New World, he was charged with mutiny and placed under arrest. He was supposed to be executed upon their arrival, but a letter from the company saved him, as the letter stated that he was to become one of the leaders. In 1607, Jamestown was founded. Smith helped secure food and resources for the first Virginians. He also created maps, which greatly benefited the settlers.

In late 1607, Smith was captured by the Powhatans. It is hard to know exactly what happened, as Smith's testimony is the only source on the following events. According to him, Pocahontas, the chief's daughter, risked her own life to save his. Some scholars think that perhaps his life was never in danger and that what took place was an adoption ceremony.

In 1608, Captain John Smith had to make some bold moves to ensure the survival of the colony. He mapped the shoreline that ran along the Chesapeake Bay, searching for food. In 1609, before the Starving Time (the winter where nearly all of the settlers of Jamestown perished), Smith was gravely injured in a gunpowder explosion and was shipped home to England. He would return to the New World, but he would never go back to Virginia.

Despite the departure of John Smith and the terrible winter of 1609/10, the settlement survived. This was due to the arrival of the relief ships that had become stranded in Bermuda. On board one of these ships was John Rolfe, who would greatly influence the future of the colony. John Rolfe receives credit for starting the tobacco industry in the colonies. Rolfe possessed tobacco seeds from the West Indies, and in 1611, he became the first person to grow tobacco commercially. He started to experiment with growing and planting them in Jamestown. The colonial leadership had spent a lot of time searching for successful goods to export. Tobacco became the first.

Keep in mind that the colonists experienced a lot of trial and error. They didn't realize that growing one crop year-round on the same soil would drain it of its nutrients. As the Virginia soil started to suffer, they had to find other ways to support their economy.

In 1619, the Virginia General Assembly began setting down rules to maximize the crop's profitability. They set up ports and warehouses, which then led to the settlement of Norfolk, Alexandria, and Richmond. The colonists shipped tobacco to England, where England's agents distributed it. Since Virginia and England relied so heavily on the crop, it reached the point where they did overgrow it. Shipping disruptions also became an issue. Remember that England never stopped being involved in conflicts. The events of the early 1700s caused tobacco prices to fluctuate. They stabilized from 1740 to 1750, but the tobacco market didn't return to its glory days. It continued to deteriorate in the 1760s and 1770s.

Tobacco growers had to adjust to the market, so they started to plant other crops. It made more sense to focus on growing food-related crops such as wheat. When the Revolutionary War broke out, the colonists were in a better position to grow food due to this move. Plus, it helped restore the soil in areas where it was drained.

John Rolfe is notable for another reason as well. Like John Smith, Rolfe encountered the famed Powhatan chief's daughter. In 1613, the English captured Pocahontas by tricking her into thinking they could make an alliance. They demanded several things from her father, and while he gathered them, Pocahontas lived with the Europeans in Virginia. While she was there, she met John Rolfe.

Rolfe's wife and child had passed away on the voyage to the New World, leaving him a widow. However, although he loved the chief's daughter, he had a hard time justifying his marriage to her; in his eyes, she was a heathen. Practically everyone in the settlement would have had the same opinion. By that point in time, though, Pocahontas had become a Christian, taking on the name Rebecca. In 1614, Rolfe put aside his moral dilemma and married her.

The Baptism of Pocahontas *(1840) by John Gadsby Chapman.*

https://commons.wikimedia.org/wiki/File:Baptism_of_Pocahontas.jpg

During ancient and colonial times (and even today to some extent), marriages helped two sides gain something politically or even financially. It does not seem as if this particular arrangement was political; by all accounts, they actually cared for each other. Nevertheless, their marriage helped to establish peace between the inhabitants of Jamestown and the natives.

In early 1615, the two had a son named Thomas. Later that year, their small family headed to England. Pocahontas (now Rebecca) was presented to the court in England. She was treated like royalty, but there is no doubt she was also seen as an oddity. They paraded her around like a princess, even though her culture did not recognize her as such. The couple was set to return to the colonies in 1617, but she passed away before seeing Virginia again.

Rolfe married yet again in 1619. Unfortunately, he didn't have the opportunity to spend the rest of his life with her. In 1622, he died, likely of natural causes. However, it is possible that he died in the Jamestown massacre. This massacre occurred due to the tensions between the Powhatans and the European settlers. Although the marriage of Pocahontas helped create peace while her father was alive, once the throne was taken by his younger brother, Opechancanough, around 1620, things changed. In March 1622, the Powhatans attacked, killing around four hundred colonists, which equates to about a third of their population. They attacked not only Jamestown but also other nearby settlements.

The conflicts between the Powhatan and the English were rough for both sides. Both sides killed the other, even women and children, and the English no longer saw the land as belonging to the Powhatan. In fact, the massacre gave the English the perfect justification for continuing to take their land. British historian Betty Wood states that "As far as the survivors...were concerned, by virtue of launching this unprovoked assault, Native Americans had forfeited any legal and moral rights they might previously have claimed to the ownership of the lands they occupied." More wars took place, such as the Third-Anglo Powhatan War of 1644. Many settlers died, but it also saw the death of Opechancanough. His death caused the end of the Powhatan uprisings. By 1684, the Powhatan Confederacy no longer existed, and the Powhatans instead lived on reservation lands.

Jamestown residents, as well as residents in all Thirteen Colonies, became the victims of many things other than Native American attacks, including the weather, disease, and food shortages. In addition, some sailed to the New World to hunt for gold. Since they focused on riches, they didn't focus on finding ways to sustain themselves.

Smith is quoted as saying, "There was no talk, no hope, no work but dig gold, wash gold, refine gold, load gold—such a bruit of GOLD that one mad fellow desired to be buried in the sands, lest they should by their art make gold of his bones!" Smith also famously said, "He that will not work shall not eat."

In addition to gold, England needed lands to expand. It needed to provide for its growing population at home. On top of this, England needed to compete with France and Spain. England had to expand trade to help the economy. The country also sought to spread its religion. Spain spread theirs in Mexico; England could do the same.

In 1642, Sir William Berkeley became the governor of Virginia. This was the year the First English Civil War broke out. While the conflict raged in England, the supporters of Charles I fled to Virginia, bringing their ideas to the colony. When Charles I was beheaded for treason in 1649, British Parliament turned on Berkeley, as he supported the Crown. From 1652 to 1659, he was forced out of the governorship. He spent that time on his Virginia plantation. In 1660, he was restored as governor.

Sir William Berkeley's time as governor experienced other problems. For example, Nathaniel Bacon led a rebellion against him. Berkeley was not responding to attacks by Native Americans efficiently enough. In addition, the economy was in a slump, the crops ceased to grow successfully, and the taxes went up. The people had had enough. In 1676, Bacon, who was Berkeley's cousin, led an attack against an Occaneechi village, killing most of the men, women, and children who lived there.

Although reforms were passed to placate Bacon and his followers, it was not enough. Bacon then led five hundred followers to Jamestown to demand the establishment of a militia in order to deal with the threat the Native Americans posed. The rebellion was a bloody moment in Virginia's history. During the rebellion, which lasted several months, buildings in Jamestown were burned to the ground. Eventually, the rebellion was subdued, with Bacon dying of dysentery in October of 1676 before the Royal Navy could arrive as backup. Berkeley returned to Jamestown at the beginning of 1677. He was relieved of the governorship and ordered to return to England to answer for his actions and the chaos that took place in Jamestown. That summer, he passed away.

Despite this stain on his time in office, Berkeley managed to accomplish several important things during his governorship. Since he was an educated man, he had an instinct for running the colony. He helped the colony experiment with crop diversification, and he also encouraged manufacturing and expansion. In addition, he had to deal with the aggressions posed by the Dutch and Native Americans, with his efforts to tamp down those aggressions slowing down as he grew older.

In the 1700s, the Virginians decided to expand their lands. The governors of Virginia during this time, which lasted from the 1730s to the 1770s, believed this was a great idea. By having settlers in the backwoods area, they would act as a buffer zone against Native American attacks. It is thought that by the 1740s, ten thousand Europeans lived in the Shenandoah Valley, a valley bounded by the Blue Ridge Mountains, the Potomac River, and the James River. As time passed, the Virginians continued pressing for more land, such as the Ohio Country. Their efforts to gain this land helped lead to the French and Indian War, which will be discussed in more detail in Chapter 8.

Shenandoah Valley *(1859-1860) by William Louis Sonntag Sr.*

https://commons.wikimedia.org/wiki/File:Shenandoah_Valley_William_Louis_Sonntag.jpeg

Several leaders of the American Revolution War hailed from Virginia, including George Washington. It was also the site of the First Continental Congress. At the Second Virginia Convention, Patrick Henry gave his famous "Give me liberty or give me death!" speech in 1775.

Chapter 7 – Life in the Colonies

Sometimes individuals who take a glance at American colonial history make assumptions. It takes time to study and understand everything that happened in the span of about three hundred years. To fully appreciate American colonial history, it's also important to take off the glasses through which we view the world today.

Colonial America didn't have cars, phones, or the internet. However, it did have ingenious, scrappy individuals and great thinkers. Colonial life in America was far different from life in the 1900s and 2000s. Thanks to Benjamin Franklin, individuals who wanted to read books could read them at the first circulating library in Philadelphia. Services like this were free for members, but even those who were not members could check out books; they just had to leave behind the money for the book, which they would get back when they returned it.

Of course, things like libraries took time to develop. Also, some educational opportunities were reserved for certain occupations and genders. Women, for instance, were often only taught enough to read the Bible in the early days of the colonial period. But everyone had a purpose, especially at this point in history. The majority of the individuals traveling to the New World were male. For several decades, the population saw an imbalance between males and females. Therefore, women were in high demand. When the settlers started having children, the ratio improved but remained unbalanced. The first census numbers show that men easily outnumbered women six to one. This makes sense. Many men were unattached when they made their way to the Americas, as the new lands supposedly promised riches and stability; it was a place where they could start and raise a family of their own.

To boost the female population, they were offered free passage to the New World. Between 1619 and 1622, tobacco brides were sent to Jamestown. In total, 144 women traveled to America, and once they got there, they were auctioned off for around 150 pounds of tobacco each, with the price going to the company who shipped the women. However, only around thirty-five of these women survived their first six years in the colonies.

Regardless, the female population increased as the Pilgrims, Puritans, and other settlers started having children on American soil. By the time the 1700s rolled around, the ratio of men to women improved; it was now three to one.

A woman's place became her home, and she was surrounded by her children. This was especially the case in New England, which makes sense since this region was mainly inhabited by the Puritans. Since women birthed the babies, it was logical that her contribution to her household and society was bearing and raising children in the Christian way. Researchers estimate that a healthy woman bore ten children in her lifetime. Evidence shows that women bore children until they reached menopause. If she could birth them, she would have them. It is believed that one out of eight women died giving birth to children.

Although modern America has a different view on motherhood and a woman's place in society, Puritan women didn't see anything wrong with how they lived. Today, we would see their position as being inferior to men, but mothers were still celebrated back then. She played an important role as the gatekeeper of her children and family. Women were also still loved, at least for the most part, by their husbands. However, they did have few rights in regard to the law and had to listen to her husband in almost all matters.

Puritan women maintained the home. They looked after the children, cooked, and cleaned. Women also had the job of weaving clothes. Men worked the land or engaged in craftsmanship. The eldest children helped look after their younger siblings, did chores, and attended church. There was not much socializing for children back then, as the Puritans were rather strict. They wanted children to be obedient, and if they stepped out of line, they would often be beaten. However, this was not done out of hate. The Puritans believed firm discipline was needed at a young age so children would grow up to be adults with a firm belief in the way God wanted the world to work. Schools were set up for children, and all children knew how to read. Typically, though, only boys learned how to write.

Some of the colonists, especially in the North and even the South, lived in the backwoods of America. For some, it might be easy to write them off as uneducated "hillbillies," a derogatory term used to refer to people in the United States who live in rural areas. The truth is the exact opposite. The colonists built their homes, worked the land, and gave birth to the next generation. Many of them were indeed educated, and the Puritans began an effort to continue that tradition in the New World.

Religious leaders did their best to make sure everyone adhered to a high moral standard. There was a tendency to drink even among the Puritans, but the degeneracy was kept to a minimum. The Puritans allowed divorces (in fact, they had the most liberal divorce laws in all of the Thirteen Colonies), but they did not happen very often. Back then, people didn't divorce for the lack of love in a marriage; rather, they could only do so in cases of infidelity or desertion. Remarrying was also common for men since they tended to outlive their wives. Several of the Founding Fathers and colonial icons remarried.

The living situation varied from region to region, but in colonial America, religion always played an important role in the lives of colonists. Women did not work alongside their husbands in New England, but in the Middle Colonies, it was common to see women working in the fields. Overall, though, women were expected to listen to their husbands, raise the children, and take care of the household.

In the early colonial period, there was not much time for extraneous activities since the colonists had to remain vigilant of potential threats to their well-being. Although the settlers encroached on the lands of the Native Americans, many of them did their best to establish peace with them. Of course, not all of the settlers did so, and not all of the natives accepted their terms of peace. The battles that took place between the natives and settlers are common events that take place when any group comes into a new land.

The colonists faced other dangers besides Native American attacks. If they didn't die from starvation, they passed away from disease. If they survived starvation, disease, and outside attacks, they still had to deal with the wildlife that lived in the New World too.

Having an educated populace to counter the problems they faced was of the utmost importance. In 1636, the Great and General Court of Massachusetts Bay Colony received a significant grant. They established Harvard in Cambridge, Massachusetts, although it would only get its name a year later. Harvard is the oldest educational institution in America. All the Ivy League educational institutions had a religious slant. Harvard's denomination leaned toward Congregational. Harvard's purpose was to educate the clergy, and its early model was based on English universities. Most of the ministers who attended Harvard went to preach in Puritan churches. Estimates show that seventeen thousand Puritans had migrated to the New World by 1636. Thus, the population needed religious leadership.

Despite competition from other universities, Harvard still remains one of the most prestigious in the United States. However, the purpose of Harvard has changed. It stopped being a place to educate clergymen and evolved into producing entrepreneurs and America's top leaders. Even today, in many cases, Harvard's dropouts have the same caliber as those who graduated, as many of them enter the technology sector.

The next colonial college in what is now the United States was not established until 1693. William and Mary College was an Anglican college, and it resided in Williamsburg, Virginia. King William III and Queen Mary II approved the charter that established the college. They deemed that the institution's purpose was to create a place for studying, philosophizing, and learning languages. This school has stayed true to its original purpose. Today, its commitment is research and learning. It also still retains ties with the British Crown.

In 1701, the Connecticut legislature helped establish Yale. Like Harvard, it leaned toward Congregational. Its religious origins could explain the intense rivalry that still takes place between Harvard and Yale in all aspects of education, from sports to student performance. Unlike Harvard, Yale moved locations a few times. Yale remained true to its Orthodox Puritan ideals, with its studies focusing on the classics. In the early 1800s, the school branched out its studies. It established its medical school in 1810. The school of divinity and theology arrived in 1822. Finally, the school established its law school in 1824.

Education in colonial America focused on the things that the communities needed. As the needs of the colonies evolved, education did too. The next school that was established was Princeton in 1746. It started as the College of New Jersey, and it leaned Presbyterian. Nine colleges were founded during the colonial period. Some of the other colleges that were built included the University of Pennsylvania in 1751, Columbia in 1754, Brown in 1764, Rutgers in 1766, and Dartmouth in 1769.

North America was established primarily by the English. Therefore, the culture that thrived throughout the colonies was English. However, many immigrants called the Thirteen Colonies home, with the most diverse populations of settlements residing in the Middle Colonies. Regardless of their differences, the colonists all held education in high regard. Thus, it makes sense that they began to establish schools. In the colonial days, education at a university level was reserved for the upper crust of society, and only men could attend. Typically, universities had around two hundred young men in attendance, which is much lower than admittance today.

Although schools were available for younger children, wealthy families often used private tutors to educate their young. This was often the case in the Southern Colonies, regardless of wealth. Its makeup was different from its New England and Middle Colonies counterparts. Since the Southern Colonies focused heavily on agriculture, the parcels of land were separated from each other. They had large cities, but oftentimes, the people would be spread out more, making them more isolated from each other. This made community schools, for the most part, impossible, so children would either be taught by their parents or tutors.

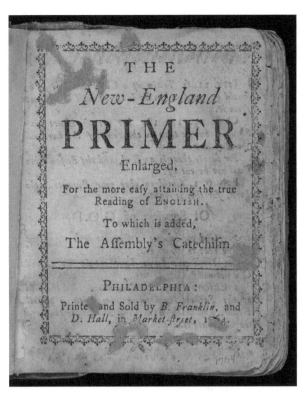

A copy of the New England Primer, which was the most popular primer to teach reading in the late 17ᵗʰ and 18ᵗʰ centuries.

The colonists throughout the New World didn't have a lot of spare time. They spent their days working the land, turning textiles into products, and preparing meals from scratch. However, there was some time for fun. Even the Puritans played games and had celebrations. Some of the most popular pastimes in the Thirteen Colonies were dancing, singing, sharing stories, and having quilting bees. Horse races were a huge source of entertainment in Virginia. Racing horses were reserved for the wealthy, as it was expensive to maintain a healthy racing horse. But everyone enjoyed the spectacle, and the landed gentry enjoyed showing their horses off. Children would play games like hopscotch, marbles, tag, and hide-and-seek. Young girls would also dress up dolls made out of corn husks.

But again, things started to change as the Europeans settled into their new home. The first generation spent their time figuring things out. The second generation learned from the first. They had the opportunity to improve the processes established by the original generation. Thus, life improved for the colonists. They accumulated land, wealth, and knowledge. They set down roots in the New World, and they influenced other parts of the world. And as time passed, people were able to focus on the arts. There were several individuals who made contributions to the arts during the colonial period.

For instance, there was John Trumbull (1756-1843). He had a diverse set of skills; he became a painter, author, and architect. Trumbull is the artist responsible for capturing the signing of the Declaration of Independence in art. He studied with Benjamin West, another influential artist of the Revolutionary period. Trumbull balanced his art with serving as a public servant. In 1794, he became John Jay's secretary; in fact, he was present when the Jay Treaty was signed. The Jay Treaty helped to avert more warfare between the United States and Great Britain.

Trumbull finally settled in New York City from 1815 to 1837. There, he maintained a small art studio. The United States Congress commissioned him to paint four paintings that would sit in the Capitol Rotunda. The paintings included *General George Washington Resigning His Commission, Surrender of Lord Cornwallis,* and *Surrender of General Burgoyne.* His *Declaration of Independence* was painted in 1818. In 1831, Benjamin Silliman set up the Trumbull Gallery at Yale, which was the first gallery established at an American educational institution.

The Declaration of Independence, July 4, 1776 *(1832) by John Trumbull.*

https://en.wikipedia.org/wiki/File:Declaration_of_Independence_(1819),_by_John_Trumbull.jpg

Charles W. Peale also painted portraits that focused on moments from the Revolutionary War. Like most American colonial icons, Peale had a modest beginning. He gained skills as a saddler, watchmaker, and silversmith. His first exposure to art was trading a saddle for painting lessons. Peale later met and received advice from John S. Copley. He even received sponsorship and had the opportunity to study under Benjamin West in London. In 1775, he moved to Philadelphia and saw his demand increase in the Middle Colonies. When the Revolutionary War broke out, he served in the militia. He saw his career suffer when he advocated for the Whigs in 1789.

Estimates show that Peale painted 1,100 portraits. His subjects included the Founding Fathers, such as George Washington, Thomas Jefferson, and Benjamin Franklin. Since he settled in Philadelphia, he had access to these great men. Peale wrote an essay in 1812 called "An Essay to Promote Domestic Happiness." Some individuals make a connection between the essay and how he posed his subjects.

Washington at Princeton *(1779) by Charles Wilson Peale.*

Benjamin West was well regarded in the art circle. Both Charles W. Peale and John S. Copley studied under him. West painted under George III, and he helped to found the Royal Academy in 1768. Before this, West studied painting in Philadelphia in 1756, and he found success painting portraits in New York City. As neoclassicism caught on, he found sponsors who helped him travel to Italy to see the art trend for himself. George III provided Benjamin West with financial support, which meant that he didn't need to make a living painting portraits anymore. Once he received this financial support, West didn't return to the United States. However, colonists traveled to London to learn from him. Thus, his influence was felt outside of London.

Self-portrait of Benjamin West *(1776).*

John S. Copley was perhaps the best painter in colonial America. He painted portraits and historical subjects. It is believed that he picked up basic skills in art from his stepfather, but no one knows for sure because there aren't many records.

Copley found that his skills lay in portraits. He posed his subjects with objects from their daily life. The technique gave more insight into the subject. For example, Copley painted the portrait of Paul Revere that is commonly found in American history textbooks. In this painting, Revere is holding a silver teapot. It was a great artistic choice. Instead of depicting the man in a heroic pose on top of a horse, Revere is portrayed as any American. He is holding one of the pots he had crafted himself.

Paul Revere *(1768) by John Singleton Copley.*

Those who commissioned portraits from Copley were often from the upper class. This isn't surprising, as portraits like this were quite expensive. The artist decided that he wanted to branch out, and he entered art shows. He showed *Boy with a Squirrel* at the Society of Artists in London in 1766. The portrait received high praise from Copley's peers.

The artist ended up leaving the colonies before the American Revolution broke out. His father-in-law was involved in the Boston Tea Party, though. In 1776, Copley established his home in London. In 1778, he started painting people and nature, such as his *Watson and the Shark*. He entered the Royal Academy in 1779, and he gained a foothold in the Romantic art movement. Some believe that his paintings in Boston were superior to those he painted in London. His deteriorating health probably played a role in the quality of the portraits.

Paintings were not only the artistic forms found in the colonies. In terms of music, it depended on the region. The people who inhabited the colonies brought their culture and customs with them. The English, French, Dutch, Swedes, and Spanish brought their music with them. Even the German population that settled in Pennsylvania integrated their customs with their surroundings. Since the British were the majority population by 1776, their culture was the most prominent.

Drumming was perhaps the most common form of music after singing. Since the colonies were all fairly religious, they often sang the Psalms. Other instruments that found their way to the colonies included the flute and fife. Most people have seen images of the drum and fife corps that marched with the soldiers during the Revolutionary War. Wooden instruments were also common, such as the recorder. Brass instruments also became prevalent, which included the trombone, trumpet, and French horn. String instruments found their way to the colonies from Europe as well. Most instruments were reserved for men. If women wanted to play instruments, they chose the harpsichord, which is an instrument similar to the piano.

A chapter on colonial life wouldn't be complete without talking about the economy. As mentioned in this book, the colonies were an extension of England (later known as Great Britain). They were not independent even though they sat an ocean away. England dictated the terms of trade. The colonists had the freedom to establish representation to help them complete daily activities, but England set down the rules in regard to major decisions.

The colonies produced crops and other items that were shipped to England. The colonists could only receive raw materials and products from England. This situation led to what is known as the triangular trade.

Although the cargo sometimes changed, essentially, English/British ships would sail to Africa with textiles, rum, and other manufactured goods. In return for these goods, the merchants would receive slaves, which they would then take to the West Indies or Thirteen Colonies. The slaves would then be exchanged, and the ships would be loaded with items for England. The triangular trade made good use of the ships and maximized resources.

Mercantilism and the triangular trade ensured that the colonies had several restrictions placed on them. They could have traded with France for better profits. However, England's military on the ground ensured that this didn't occur. Nevertheless, contraband was smuggled both in and out of the colonies. The colonists were a shrewd people and bribed customs officials to look the other way.

Chapter 8 – Threats and Conflicts That England Faced: The Lead-up to the American Revolution

During the colonial period, many major wars took place. Some of them have been mentioned above, such as the English Civil Wars. The wars covered in this chapter took place later, with the first one taking place in the late 17th century. The Nine Years' War, also known as the War of the League of Augsburg or the War of the Grand Alliance, took place from 1688 to 1697. This conflict was between France on one side and England, the Netherlands, and the Austrian Habsburgs, to name just a few, on the other. King Louis XIV of France continued his attempts at expansion across the Rhine. He sought to pressure the Holy Roman Empire but was met with pushback from England.

Although many powers faced off against France, Louis XIV's men fought well. However, in 1696, the country was suffering from a poor economy. The other powers were also tired of the fighting and suffering on the economic front. Peace was agreed to in 1697.

However, the Treaty of Ryswick didn't completely end the ill feelings the countries had toward each other.

The conflict continued between the English and French and between the Habsburgs and the Spanish Bourbons. During this period, who took the throne mattered. Alliances were still formed through marriage; thus, some heirs carried French blood while others carried Spanish. This became a problem because King Charles II of Spain (r. 1665–1700) didn't produce any heirs.

This culminated in another major war: the War of the Spanish Succession. The war lasted from 1701 to 1714. When Charles II passed away, the throne was open. It essentially boiled down to either a Habsburg or a Bourbon taking the crown. Before his death, Charles named Philip of Anjou, Louis XIV's grandson, who was a Bourbon, as his heir. If he did not accept, Charles II wanted the throne to go to Archduke Charles, the son of Holy Roman Emperor Leopold I. The issue was made complicated due to the various treaties that had been signed in the decade prior to Charles's death. War would have likely happened no matter who took the throne. Britain entered the war because it feared French expansion.

The French did well at the beginning of the war, but they began to lose their grip by 1706. The British forces managed to win battles against France, and the French started losing their strongholds in lands outside its borders. For instance, France found itself forced out of the Low Countries and Italy. Nevertheless, Philip was still made king. In 1711, Archduke Charles, the other contender for the throne, became the Holy Roman emperor. There was no need to continue the war, so peace talks were soon sought. In 1713, the countries agreed to the Treaty of Utrecht. Philip was acknowledged as the king of Spain. Britain, on the other hand, received territories like Gibraltar and gained trade agreements in the Spanish colonies in the New World. Due to these developments, Britain was now the leading commercial power.

The War of the Austrian Succession was another conflict between the Bourbons and Habsburgs. It took place from 1740 to 1748. This time, it was Holy Roman Emperor Charles VI (the same Archduke Charles involved in the War of the Spanish Succession) who passed away. His daughter, Maria Theresa, was in line for the throne, but other powers, such as France and Prussia, saw a chance to challenge the Habsburgs' power. This was because the original pact of succession saw the throne first going to the female heirs of Charles's older brother, Joseph I. The opposing powers used this as a pretext to start a war.

Frederick II of Prussia invaded Silesia in December 1740, kicking off the war. Many European powers got sucked into the conflict. The French and Spanish sided with the Prussians against the Austrians, who had the support of the British and the Dutch. France made inroads in the Austrian Netherlands, but Austria was able to stop the Spanish from spreading into Italy again. In the meantime, the Royal Navy had blockaded the French, creating dire economic conditions in regard to trade.

The Treaty of Aix-la-Chapelle, which was signed in 1748, ended the conflict. It allowed Maria Theresa and her husband to take the throne as planned. Prussia got to keep Silesia, but most of the other territories that had been taken during the war were returned to their previous owners.

These succession wars took place in Europe. But at times, they spread over into the Thirteen Colonies. For instance, during the War of the Spanish Succession, Queen Anne's War took place. In 1701, the three big powers of England, Spain, and France began asserting their control over North America. The British won the war in 1713, with the French ceding several of their territories in the north to Britain, such as Hudson Bay and Newfoundland.

What European occupation looked like at the beginning of Queen Anne's War.

During the War of the Austrian Succession, the North American continent saw King George's War break out. In 1744, once France heard of the war taking place in Europe, it soon acted out against the nearby British. Both sides raided the other's villages and forts. Like in Queen Anne's War, the colonists were assisted by Native Americans. This war ended in 1748 with the Treaty of Aix-la-Chapelle; everything went back to the way it had been before the war.

But perhaps the best-known American colonial war is the French and Indian War, which started in 1754. This is considered to be the North American theater of the Seven Years' War, which actually began two years later in 1756. It was a significant war, as it allowed Britain and its colonies to obtain the Canadian areas that the French had settled, as well as Florida from Spain.

Map of European occupation in 1750.

The French presence has not been touched on much in this book, but they had a strong foothold in present-day Canada. As time passed, they spread westward, going as far as Wisconsin and parts of North Dakota. The French also laid claim to Louisiana, which was a highly desired territory due to its access to the Mississippi River.

Water sources were important for everyone settling in the New World. As such, the Ohio River became a focal point of conflict. In 1753, a young George Washington (who would become the first president of the United States) was sent to Ohio to protect British interests. The French were unwilling to engage in diplomatic talks, so Washington moved back south to inform the British of what he had seen.

In 1754, the first conflict of the war broke out. Both sides relied on Native Americans to augment their forces, but France certainly depended on them more. Population-wise, the British outnumbered the French by over one million; the British had around two million people, while the French had sixty thousand.

That same year, George Washington suffered his first defeat at Fort Necessity in what is today Pennsylvania; in fact, it was the only battle in which he ever surrendered. The weather, lack of equipment, and the likelihood that no reinforcements were going to arrive to aid the battle all led the young major to surrender the fort to the Canadians.

The war ebbed back and forth at the beginning, but by 1757, the British settlers were doing rather poorly. William Pitt helped turn things around. Pitt, who was the Leader of the House of Commons and the Secretary of State, understood the importance of defending the colonies against all invaders. He requested a lot of money to finance the British side of the battle. In regards to the war in Europe, Pitt began financing the Prussian forces. In regards to the war in North America, he sent forces to help conquer Canada. France, on the other hand, did not want to waste their valuable resources by sending them to the New World.

The British managed to beat the French in several key spots in Canada. They gained the most momentum when they defeated the French in Quebec in 1759. In 1760, Spain joined forces with France in the French and Indian War to protect its interests in the New World. However, it was not enough, as the British ended up winning the war.

The Treaty of Paris ended this war and the Seven Years' War in 1763. Spain lost Florida, but France gave it Louisiana instead. France lost all of its territories east of the Mississippi River.

Although the fighting with France and Spain subsided, it didn't stop with others. Immediately after the French and Indian War, the colonists near Ohio experienced Pontiac's War. Chief Pontiac from the Odawa tribe managed to unite several groups of natives. They destroyed forts and killed civilians. For instance, in 1764, a school teacher and ten children were scalped in a terrible massacre. However, the British were guilty of atrocities as well, including the killing of civilians. They offered rewards for the scalps of Native Americans for anyone above the age of ten, including women.

It was also during this war that the legendary smallpox blanket infection took place. At the Battle of Fort Pitt, which took place in 1763, the colonists were looking at a defeat. Some of the leaders thought about sending infected blankets to lower the number of Native Americans at their doors. William Trent, the commander of the fort, wrote, "We gave them two Blankets and an Handkerchief out of the Small Pox Hospital. I hope it will have the desired effect." However, the items that were sent to the natives most likely didn't have the desired effect Trent was hoping for. Still, scholars point to this incident as proof that colonists deliberately infected Native Americans throughout the colonization period. Whether this actually occurred is unknown.

This war ended in 1766 in a stalemate. Boundary lines were redrawn, recognizing the Native Americans' rights to the land, while the Native Americans recognized British sovereignty. However, this led to resentment in the colonists; they had just fought a hard war against the French for the lands in the Great Lakes region; now, they could no longer settle them? It is believed the results of this war helped contribute to the breakout of the American Revolution.

All of this fighting continued adding to Britain's debt. They leaned heavily on British bankers for financing. King George III made the decision that the Thirteen Colonies would have to provide resources to pay down the debt. After all, they had become safer as a result of Britain's victories. Logically, some of the debt belonged to them too.

Chapter 9 – The Road to Revolution

The colonists officially declared their independence from Britain on July 4th, 1776. On that day, they became Americans and formed the United States of America.

However, the path to freedom wasn't easy. The debates over whether to separate from the Motherland lasted several months. Communication was slow. Letter writing and traveling on horseback dominated these days, not smartphones, the internet, and cars.

The seeds for independence were planted fairly early on. In 1651, the Navigation Acts were passed to curtail trade. In those days, the Dutch controlled maritime trade, and England sought to change that by ensuring only ships that were manned with mostly Englishmen could transport goods from the American colonies. Historians believe the economic impact of these acts was minor but that they were the start of political tensions between the colonies and England.

The colonists learned how to survive on their own without help from the English, which created a separate identity from the mainland. The English sought to get rid of this kind of thinking, which was one of the reasons why the Dominion of New England was created. As you now know, the Dominion ultimately wasn't successful, as the colonial governments took back control.

In 1733, Britain passed the Molasses Act. The act imposed a tax on molasses and sugar that arrived from colonies that were not owned by Britain. It had to protect its sugar interests in the West Indies, as the sugarcane growers faced intense competition from the French. Thankfully, this act was not enforced well. New England depended on molasses to make rum, which was a large industry in that region. Smuggling increased, and the colonists simply refused to pay the tax.

About thirty years later, the Sugar Act was enacted. Although this act lowered the tax on molasses and sugar, it increased the enforcement of the law. At this point, the Thirteen Colonies were in a depression, and it was easy for the colonists to point to the law as a way to keep them dependent on Britain.

Both Britain and the colonies were feeling the effects of the Seven Years' War and the French and Indian War. It is easy to see why Britain demanded so much from the colonists. To the British government, the colonies were an investment, and an investment should show returns. It was costly to protect the colonists from the Native Americans, French, and Spanish. It was only right that the colonists helped share that burden.

However, the Thirteen Colonies were separated from Britain by an ocean, which allowed the colonists to develop a form of independence that the Crown could not have imagined. In 1764, though, the colonists were not as concerned about taxation without representation as they were about the negative impact the act would have on their industries.

The Sugar Act introduced an indirect tax, which means that molasses had the tax added to it by the time it reached the market. The Stamp Act, however, introduced a direct tax. It was passed in 1765, and it is safe to say the colonists did not approve of the measure. Any paper product had to have a stamp on it—including playing cards. And it could not be paid for in colonial money; it had to be paid for in British currency.

This time around, it was not the tax itself that upset the colonists; it was the fact that they had no representation in British Parliament. Even though these restrictions angered them, many of the colonists still attempted to make amends with Britain. Thomas Jefferson wrote a list of grievances, as he hoped Britain would offer some compromises. However, it couldn't compromise on the taxes since the country was in debt from fighting battles on several fronts.

On top of this, the Quartering Acts were passed later that year. British soldiers were still being stationed in the colonies even though there were no real threats to the colonists at this point. Britain ordered the colonists to provide them with housing and food.

The Stamp Act led to riots and stamp burning. It also led to the harassment of British officials. The colonists were so serious about protesting the Stamp Act that it led to the creation of the Sons of Liberty. In an ironic twist, the colonists took their group name from a speech given by Isaac Barré in British Parliament in 1765. He called the colonists who wouldn't cooperate with the new taxes the "sons of liberty." He believed the people in the Americas were as loyal as any other subject but that they sought liberties that had been denied to them for so long.

The colonists managed to organize themselves in secret extremely well. They knew that getting caught was not an option. If they did, they would find themselves in prison without bail or a fair hearing. Researchers believe that the Sons of Liberty was an offshoot of the Loyal Nine. In 1765, nine Bostonians formed the Loyal Nine in secrecy to protest the Stamp Act. These nine men all joined the Sons of Liberty. The Sons of Liberty counted Samuel Adams (who founded the group), Benjamin Edes, John Hancock, Paul Revere, Charles Peale, and Benedict Arnold as members. It also had a few chapters, with the two biggest ones found in Boston and New York.

The Boston chapter was the first one, and its members met in Hanover Square next to what was dubbed the Liberty Tree.

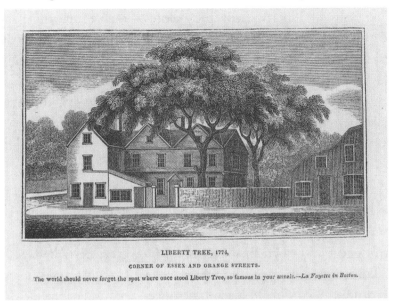

LIBERTY TREE, 1774,

CORNER OF ESSEX AND ORANGE STREETS.

The world should never forget the spot where once stood Liberty Tree, so famous in your annals.—*La Fayette in Boston.*

An illustration of the Liberty Tree (1825). The Liberty Tree was felled by Loyalists in 1775.

https://commons.wikimedia.org/wiki/File:Houghton_AC8_Sn612_825h_-_Liberty_Tree.jpg

Remember that the colonists who resisted Britain's rule didn't have access to the internet, computers, or vehicles. Instead, they used pamphlets, petitions, and assemblies to share their thoughts. Some say that the colonists used propaganda to motivate their peers. In addition, some historians view the Sons of Liberty as extremists. However, revolutions are rarely civil.

It is true that the Sons of Liberty resorted to extreme civil disobedience. For example, Andrew Oliver received a letter asking him to present himself at the Liberty Tree. Oliver was the new collector of stamps, and the colonists immediately asked him to resign in public. The letter stated that as long as he resigned, he would be treated with respect, leaving one to wonder what would have happened if he had not resigned. A crowd of two thousand people showed up at the Liberty Tree. When Oliver resigned, the public cheered and left him alone. The Sons of Liberty also burned records and looted officials' homes to make their point.

The Sons of Liberty made the colonists realize that the issue at hand wasn't about taxes; it was the fact that Britain had too much control over the colonists, who had proven time and again that they could handle themselves. Something had to change, and the Sons of Liberty were a cog that made that happen. In 1766, the Stamp Act was repealed. At the same time, the Declaratory Act was passed, which asserted Britain's right to pass binding laws on its colonies. Nevertheless, the colonists were happy with their progress.

Their happiness did not last for long. The Townshend Acts were passed only a few months later. The mastermind behind the Townshend Acts was Charles Townshend. There is no doubt that Townshend had a solid financial mind. However, he lacked political tact. Townshend also had the ability to give beautiful speeches even while drunk. According to legend, he once gave a speech while drunk on champagne in 1767. Townshend passed away a few months after Parliament passed his four resolutions (one of the Townshend Acts, the Vice Admiralty Court Act, was passed after his death). Thus, he didn't receive the opportunity to see his resolutions unfold.

The first Townshend Act was the New York Restraining Act. As the name hints, this act was aimed at New York. The colony refused to comply with the Quartering Act of 1765. Under this new act, the New York Assembly could not gather until the Quartering Act was honored. Before the act could be implemented, though, New York began paying for the soldiers.

The next resolution was the Revenue Act, which was designed to help put money into Britain's coffers. The Revenue Act placed taxes on glass, paper, paint, and tea. In addition, a person's private property could be searched to see if there were any smuggled goods. Not even people living in Britain were subjected to such violations, so the colonists protested against this measure.

The following act was the Indemnity Act. The British East India Company saw reduced taxes on exports of tea to Britain. Britain could then export the tea to the colonists at a lower price. The Dutch were a formidable trade competitor to Britain when it came to tea. They smuggled tea into the colonies, so Britain sought to put a stop to it. The act was supposed to make British tea more attractive to the colonists than tea from other countries.

The final Townshend resolution was the Commissioners of Customs Act. A new customs board was created in the colonies, which was supposed to enforce taxes and shipping regulations. Before this, Britain had to oversee these kinds of things from Europe. With a direct presence in the colonies, it made it harder for the colonists to skip out on paying taxes.

Eventually, the Townshend Acts led to a British military buildup in the Thirteen Colonies. These troops only added tension among the colonists, who saw the troops as a threat. This led to the pivotal incident of the Boston Massacre.

In early March 1770, a mob gathered around the Boston Custom House. Around fifty people gathered around the small British presence. They threw objects and shouted and taunted the soldiers standing guard. One of the soldiers was knocked down, and he angrily shot into the crowd. This was followed by several more volleys, which were never ordered by the captain. Five colonists died, with two of them dying afterward.

A 19ᵗʰ-century lithograph of Paul Revere's engraving.

https://commons.wikimedia.org/wiki/File:Boston_Massacre,_03-05-1770_-_NARA_-_518262.jpg

That same year, British Parliament did away with all of the extra taxes except for the one on tea. This helped appease the colonists somewhat, although the Sons of Liberty continued to agitate for independence.

One of the most influential Sons of Liberty was Samuels Adams, who remains one of the most important figures of colonial America and the Revolutionary War. He was a cousin of John Adams (the second president of the United States), but the two differed in their approach toward independence. John Adams was determined to remain civil, and he worked within the law.

Although Samuel Adams was an agitator and a fan of mob violence, he did attend Harvard and studied law for a brief time, so he understood the underlying issue the American colonists were facing: no representation in Parliament. He attempted to become an entrepreneur but ended up becoming a tax collector instead. However, he often refused to complete the duties of his job and didn't collect the new taxes. Samuel Adams also served as a Continental Congress delegate and signed the Declaration of Independence.

Other well-known members of the Sons of Liberty include John Hancock, Paul Revere, and Benedict Arnold.

John Hancock was a threat to British power. He successfully riled up crowds against the taxes. His efforts led him to become one of the signers of the Declaration of Independence; in fact, he was the first one to sign it.

When John Hancock's uncle passed away, he inherited his shipping business. He led a lavish lifestyle, but he was also generous with his money. Hancock first entered the political fray in 1765. Around this time, the taxes started to hit home for the colonists. It makes sense that Hancock was so opposed to the British taxes since he would have experienced the effects firsthand due to his shipping business. Thus, protests got under way. Boston became the "Cradle of Liberty." The Boston Tea Party, the Boston Massacre, and the seizure of Hancock's ship all gave the colonists a common cause around which to rally.

In 1775, Hancock was voted as the president of the Continental Congress, which met in Philadelphia. The Continental Congress chose George Washington to serve as its commander of the Continental Army. Hancock's wealth came in handy here, as he used it to fund the army and Congress.

Paul Revere is best known for his famous "Midnight Ride" in April 1775. However, both he became involved in the Sons of Liberty, he was a prosperous silversmith and engraver, and he continued his rise into the upper ranks of society during the American Revolution. He was unable to become a part of the gentry, but his Midnight Ride ensured that his name lasted to the modern age.

Revere's mission to deliver news of the British movements was secret, so he never shouted the famous words, "The British are coming!" He rode through the night, with around forty men joining him by the end of it. Revere reached Lexington around midnight, and after discussing matters with Samuel Adams and John Hancock, they decided the British would attack Concord first. Revere headed out, but he was captured along the way. One of the three riders who made the trip to Concord, Samuel Prescott, managed to elude capture and made it to Concord. (The other rider, William Dawes, was not captured, but he did not complete the ride due to falling off his horse.)

In many ways, the most famous colonists were ordinary men who did extraordinary things. Americans remember Paul Revere's ride thanks to Henry Wadsworth Longfellow's poem, which is not historically accurate. For instance, the poem says that the lanterns hung in the Old North Church were placed there for Revere to begin his ride. In reality, he was the one who had the lantern system set up.

Perhaps the most infamous Son of Liberty was Benedict Arnold. Most Americans today have heard of this man. If someone uses the name, they're referring to the word traitor. But Arnold actually started off as a hero to the colonists. It seems like his ego got in the way. Other men continued to win the hearts and minds of the colonists, such as George Washington. Thus, they started to receive glory and promotions. Arnold was passed up for promotions, and he felt like he was not being recognized for his services.

It perhaps did not help that Arnold's second marriage was to a woman whose father was loyal to the British cause. He started to communicate with the British through her family's contacts, with those contacts asking him to surrender West Point in New York, of which he had command, in 1780. However, the colonists captured Major John André, a British spy, who had papers revealing Arnold's plans of surrender. Arnold then received a commission with the British army, and after the war, he spent the rest of his days in England.

Before Arnold's betrayal, George Washington greatly admired the man. Although Washington was not a part of the Sons of Liberty, he deserves a special mention, as he was not only the commander of the Continental Army during the Revolutionary War but also became the first president of the United States. He did not approve of what the

British were doing in the colonies, and he accepted the roles that were thrust upon him.

The number of things that Washington accomplished after the Revolutionary War are many. He wasn't an inventor like Benjamin Franklin, and he wasn't a prolific writer like Thomas Jefferson. However, he contributed as a leader. He set the bar for leadership and the number of terms a US president should serve. Washington passed away at the age of sixty-seven, but he lived a full life. He had military accomplishments and leadership accomplishments of which many leaders could only dream.

Benjamin Franklin was another Founding Father who wasn't involved in the Sons of Liberty. He had perhaps the most communication with British Parliament. Franklin was in Britain as a diplomat when some of the restrictive measures, like the Stamp Act, were being passed. He testified against this act, saying, "Suppose a military force sent into America; they will find nobody in arms; what are they then to do. They cannot force a man to take stamps who chooses to do without them. They will not find a rebellion; they may indeed make one." Shortly after the American Revolution began, Franklin cut his ties to Britain and headed home to aid in the war. He served on the Continental Congress and helped draft the Declaration of Independence.

These men all played an important role in the lead-up to the war. But it must be noted that the war effort would have never succeeded if it weren't for the many ordinary people who sought independence. Perhaps the most famous act of civil disobedience that took place during the road to the Revolutionary War was the Boston Tea Party in 1773. This was a result of the Tea Act, which was passed to deal with the problem of smuggling. The British East India Company could now ship tea directly to the colonists, but the people still had to pay the tea tax. The people did everything they could to protest this.

On the evening of December 16th, 1773, a group of colonists, mainly men from the Sons of Liberty, dressed as Native Americans and destroyed ninety-two thousand pounds of tea at Boston harbor. The loss would equate to about one million dollars today. The British tea stained the water, and the colonists found themselves in hot water. However, they didn't care about the feelings of the British anymore. Most of them had already made up their minds.

An engraving titled **Boston Tea Party** *(1789).*

https://commons.wikimedia.org/wiki/File:Boston_Tea_Party_w.jpg

After the Boston Tea Party, British Parliament passed the Intolerable Acts in 1774, directly retaliating against the colonists for their rebellion. Parliament started with the Boston Port Act. Since Boston was ground zero for the destruction of so much tea, they received the harshest punishment. The port was closed until the tea that was destroyed was repaid. Next, Parliament passed the Massachusetts Government Act. This made the colony a crown colony, which meant that the people could no longer represent themselves. The colony's leadership was replaced with appointed representatives from Britain. Only one town meeting could take place a year unless the people had the approval of the governor.

The Administration of Justice Act helped get English troops and officials out of trouble. Some of them behaved in careless ways; thus, the colonists had the right to put them on trial. However, this act allowed the troops to travel to England and face trial there. Obviously, this was a way to help them avoid punishment. However, it was rare for a British official to face an unfair trial. Even those involved in the Boston Massacre had fair representation. Many, including George Washington, called this the "Murder Act," as it essentially let the British in North America get away with murder.

The Intolerable Acts also introduced another Quartering Act. The previous one had been mostly ignored, but this one stated that the governor should house soldiers in buildings that were unoccupied. A popular myth is that the British made the colonists take soldiers into their own private homes. The act did not require such a thing to occur, and this only happened on a small scale.

One other act proved "intolerable" to the colonists, although it was not officially a part of the previous acts. The Quebec Act was passed by British Parliament in 1774. Its goal was to expand the Province of Quebec into much of what is now the Midwest. This essentially voided the colonists' hard-won French and Indian War, as it granted concessions to the French still living there. It also limited the Ohio Company's claims on the land, which it utilized for the fur trade industry. In addition, it restored the power of the Catholic Church in the region. The colonists saw how generous British Parliament was to the French while they were being oppressed as British subjects.

Later that year, the First Continental Congress met, and the rest is now history. The following year, the colonists faced off against the British in the Battles of Lexington and Concord, kicking off the American Revolutionary War. This war is heavily featured in many history books, so we will end the period of American colonial history here. However, some scholars push the end date of colonial America to the Declaration of Independence, which declared America's independence from Britain. Some even go as far as the end of the American Revolution, which concluded in 1783.

Conclusion

Over four hundred years ago, Jamestown was founded. It is astounding to see how much progress has been made in that city and throughout all of what is now the United States. The United States of America saw several demographic changes during the 1900s. Its economy, value system, and laws have seen several changes too.

In fact, for Americans today, it's difficult to imagine that such disputes occurred between a country that is often seen as the greatest ally of the US. By taking a look at American colonial history, it's possible to understand the sacrifices that were made by the Founding Fathers and the other colonists. Hundreds of thousands of men volunteered to fight for independence, and many risked jail time to get out from under the thumb of the British Crown.

However, their actions would not have been possible without the early colonists, those men and women who established infrastructure and government systems that allowed the colonies to flourish into a place where revolutionary ideals could take hold. These men and women had to learn how to adapt to their environment, which was filled with enemies and diseases that claimed many lives. American colonial history also shows the ingenuity of the colonists who left the comforts of home behind. They set down the foundation for the Industrial Revolution, future infrastructure, and innovations.

Even though the colonists engaged in reprehensible acts, especially when looking at them from a modern viewpoint, it is clear to see that they achieved many impressive accomplishments. Studying this fascinating period of history allows people to not only acknowledge past mistakes but also to find inspiration from the dedication and ingenuity of the early European settlers of the United States of America.

There is so much more to learn about colonial America, and we highly encourage you to look at the list of suggested reading to continue your education on this captivating time period.

Here's another book by Captivating History that you might like

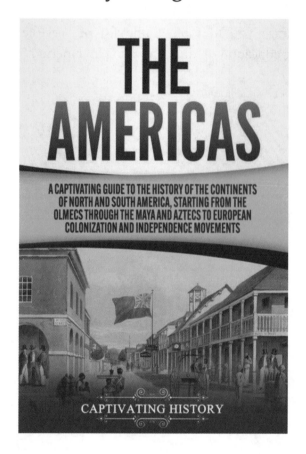

Free Bonus from Captivating History
(Available for a Limited time)

Hi History Lovers!

Now you have a chance to join our exclusive history list so you can get your first history ebook for free as well as discounts and a potential to get more history books for free! Simply visit the link below to join.

Captivatinghistory.com/ebook

Also, make sure to follow us on Facebook, Twitter and Youtube by searching for Captivating History.

Suggested Reading

Alan Taylor. *American Colonies: The Settling of North America.* 1955.

Charles C. Mann. *1493: Uncovering the New World Columbus Created.* 2011.

William Bradford (Editor: Harold Paget). *Of Plymouth Plantation.* 2016.

David Hackett Fischer. *Albion's Seed: Four British Folkways in America.* 1989.

William Cronon. *Changes in the Land: Indians, Colonists, and the Ecology of New England.* 2003.

Stephen Brumwell. *White Devil: A True Story of War, Savagery and Vengeance in Colonial America.* 2006.

Don Jordon & Michael Walsh. *White Cargo: The Forgotten History of Britain's White Slaves in America.* 2008.

William Dalrymple. *The Anarchy: The East India Company, Corporate Violence, and the Pillage of an Empire.* 2019.

Cokie Roberts. *Founding Mothers: The Women Who Raised Our Nation.* 2005.

Marilynne K. Roach. *Six Women of Salem: The Untold Story of the Accused and Their Accusers in the Salem Witch Trials.* 2013.

James Horn. *1619: Jamestown and the Forging of American Democracy.* 2018.